THE
HARBINGER

COMPANION
With STUDY GUIDE

THE
HARBINGER
COMPANION
With STUDY GUIDE

JONATHAN CAHN

Most Charisma House Book Group products are available at special quantity discounts for bulk purchase for sales promotions, premiums, fund-raising, and educational needs. For details, write Charisma House Book Group, 600 Rinehart Road, Lake Mary, Florida 32746, or telephone (407) 333-0600.

The Harbinger Companion With Study Guide by Jonathan Cahn
Published by FrontLine
Charisma Media/Charisma House Book Group
600 Rinehart Road
Lake Mary, Florida 32746
www.charismahouse.com

Unless otherwise noted, all Scripture quotations are from the New King James Version of the Bible. Copyright © 1979, 1980, 1982 by Thomas Nelson, Inc., publishers. Used by permission.

Scripture quotations marked NIV are from the Holy Bible, New International Version. Copyright © 1973, 1978, 1984, International Bible Society. Used by permission.

Cover design by Justin Evans
Design Director: Bill Johnson

Visit the author's website at www.hopeoftheworld.org.

Library of Congress Cataloging-in-Publication Data:
An application to register this book for cataloging has been submitted to the Library of Congress.
International Standard Book Number: 978-1-62136-245-6
E-book ISBN: 978-1-62136-246-3

While the author has made every effort to provide accurate telephone numbers and Internet addresses at the time of publication, neither the publisher nor the author assumes any responsibility for errors or for changes that occur after publication.

13 14 15 16 17 — 9 8 7 6 5 4 3
Printed in the United States of America

To you, the reader, we pray this guide helps you to go deeper into the mysteries, the revelations, and calling of *The Harbinger* in the hope that you, your group, or your congregation will respond to everything that God is calling you to be and do, that you will be used as a light in prayer, in repentance, and in the spreading of the Word for salvation, revival, and redemption for such a time as this.

ת א

Contents

A WORD *From* JONATHAN

THE MESSAGE OF *The Harbinger* has taken on a life of its own. It has been that way from the beginning. Even before I committed it to written form as a book, it was as if the message was meant to spread. From the first moment that I shared the first part of the revelations that would become *The Harbinger*, the message began to go forth. The recording of that teaching began to spread across the country. People held showings of it in their homes for guests; churches began showing it in their services. There was a growing call among those who had seen or heard it that the message had to go forth to the nation and its leaders.

When I finally sat down to write what would become *The Harbinger* in the form it now appears, it was almost as if the book was writing itself. The words just flowed out, as if the message was meant, from the beginning, to go forth in book form. I had never written a book before, and as the leader of several ministries, I had little spare time to devote to it, and yet in a short time *The Harbinger* was done.

I then had to decide what to do next. I was told that most books are never published and most publishers aren't interested in first-time authors they know nothing about. That same week, on my way to Dallas, in the airport in Charlotte, North Carolina, I lifted *The Harbinger* to the Lord, asking Him to send forth His word by His arm. As I opened my eyes, something quite supernatural happened that caused *The Harbinger* to go forth as a book. I didn't do anything but close my eyes and bow my head—but the word had to go forth.

Because of all this—the message itself, the way it came, and the way it went forth—I had no doubt that it would reach many people. But I didn't expect it to happen so quickly. *The Harbinger* was released as a book in the first days of January 2012. That first week it became a *New York Times* best seller. Now, as I write this, many months later, it still goes forth as a national best seller. Those who know more about these things than I do have told me it's become a phenomenon.

I cannot remember a day that's gone by since the book came out that we haven't received messages from around the country from people whose lives are being changed by it. *The Harbinger* is being preached in pulpits across the nation. Bible study groups and book clubs are focusing on it. Movements of repentance and prayer have been inspired and started up because of it. Massive amounts of people from outside the evangelical faith are reading it. People are repenting, people are consecrating their lives, and people are coming to the Lord.

Many have felt that the message of *The Harbinger* needs to go forth to those in government. That too is happening. We've now received reports, for instance, that in one state every member of the legislature, including the governor, has received a copy of the book. *The Harbinger* has even reached Capitol Hill. Several members of Congress, senators and representatives, have sent word concerning the book. One well-known member of the House of Representatives has reported that something is stirring on Capitol Hill, and it's because of the book. Another very famous member of Congress read the book and got in touch expressing a strong burden for America's future; he came to New York City specifically to pray at Ground Zero.

This all connects with a strong sense felt among believers across the nation, namely that America is in deep crisis and in danger. *The Harbinger* reveals that this is not just a feeling but reality. The message of *The Harbinger* has gone forth at the same time that this sense of crisis and danger among believers has greatly intensified in urgency.

From the time *The Harbinger* has been released up to the time of this writing, the mainstream of American culture has continued to move ever farther from God and the ways of God. At the same time, the very deep and growing sense of crisis and alarm among believers has led to more and more movements of prayer.

And just as ominously, since *The Harbinger* came out, what the book foreshadowed is actually coming true. The harbingers are continuing. There is not here space to go into it, but suffice it to say, the mystery, the pattern, and the progression are continuing.

Given the overall direction of American culture before and after 9/11, people have asked me if there is any hope for the nation. In view of the message of *The Harbinger*, how can there be any hope? It's just the opposite. Only if there were *no* harbingers, *no* signs, and *no* warnings, would there be no hope. A warning implies the possibility of response, of heeding the warning. If the harbingers are signs, then so is the fact that what was deemed "the miracle of 9/11," the saving of St. Paul's Chapel, happened through the Sycamore of Ground Zero, one of the Nine Harbingers. This underscores a point—the purpose of the harbingers, and the purpose of *The Harbinger*, is not to consign a nation to judgment but to warn it, to wake it up, that it might not be judged.

The doctor who tells his patient he is fine, when he has a potential disease, is giving the patient no hope. But the doctor who reveals the disease warns the man and tells him what he must do if he wants to live is the one who gives hope. In the same way, the purpose of an alarm is not to bring danger to the one hearing it but to save the one hearing it from danger. *The Harbinger* is this, not only the revealing of ancient mysteries, the uncovering of a biblical template of judgment, and not a trumpet call, the sounding of an alarm, but a book of hope. As with the harbingers themselves, that is the purpose.

What is the hope? For the one who doesn't know the Lord, the hope is salvation. For America, the call is to return. And for those who do know the Lord, it is the hope to come to God in humility, prayer, intercession, and repentance, and to rise to the call of being lights to the world, even lights to America. The hope is revival. How much is needed to turn the course of a nation or to avert judgment? In the case of Sodom, it was only ten people. We don't know the answer. So all the more, we must turn and seek.

Because of the massive response and interest surrounding *The Harbinger* and the demand for more concerning it, I have been asked to write and help put together a companion to the book as well as a study guide. The following work is the result. It consists of a full thirteen-week course of deeper study designed for individuals, for groups, and for classes and congregations. It is constructed to guide those who want more into deeper exploration into the mysteries of *The Harbinger* and the biblical foundations of those mysteries, deeper insight into current events and what is happening before our eyes, and the application of the message and call of *The Harbinger* into a deeper relationship with God, repentance, consecration, anointing, and revival.

In addition to deeper study are special features and articles for those who want more—including:

- A guided tour of *The Harbinger*
- The most often asked questions about *The Harbinger*
- How the message went forth to the nation
- The key biblical figures
- Who is the prophet?
- The seals and the seal behind the seals
- Signs of the end
- Where is America in end-time prophecy?
- And more

For you who are now reading this, I pray it will be a blessing to you.

And most of all I pray that God's will for your life will be fulfilled and, through your reading and studying this book, that God will strengthen you, encourage you, edify you, consecrate you, appoint you, and empower you for all that He has called for your life; that the word will spread and the trumpet will sound through your life; and that He will have His appointed will fulfilled for such a time as this. I thank the Lord for your prayers as well.

May the Lord bless and keep you!

In His love and service,

—*JONATHAN*

Introduction

HOW *to* USE THIS COMPANION WITH STUDY GUIDE

Welcome to this companion and study guide to *The Harbinger* by Jonathan Cahn. This companion was written for individuals or groups who want to go deeper in their understanding of the mysteries in *The Harbinger* and to respond to the call of God for America and for the individual.

Section I (chapters 1–13) comprises a full exploration, teaching, and study with questions designed to guide the reader into the revelations of the book. This can be done in a thirteen-week class or course, with the last week comprising a time of prayer and application.

Section II (chapters 14–26) consists of special features that relate to the subjects, issues, and mysteries surrounding *The Harbinger*.

Everyone reading *The Harbinger Companion* or participating in the study should first read *The Harbinger* since the companion is based on it and will not make sense without it. This will greatly enhance your personal discovery, study, and prayer time. For the fullest teaching of the mysteries, purchase *The Harbinger: The Full Revelation*, the eight-CD or DVD album and accompanying materials. (See the back of the book for more information on how to obtain these resources.)

Suggested Uses

Individual study

The Harbinger Companion With Study Guide is made for individual reading and use. Here are some simple steps for getting the most out of it.

- Read *The Harbinger* and listen to the CDs or watch the DVDs.

- Read each chapter of this companion guide.

- Look up Scripture references.

- Answer questions at the end of each chapter, exploring the scriptures as you do.

- Write down and apply the mission points at the end of each study section.

Bible studies and small groups

The Harbinger Companion With Study Guide is also made for use in Bible studies and small groups. Here are some simple steps for the one leading the group.

- Leader: Have everyone first read *The Harbinger* and obtain a copy of the study guide (*The Harbinger Companion*) so that they can fully participate, explore, fill in the answers, and do the applications for each week.

- Prepare weekly teachings based on the chapters and scriptures in this companion (5–20 minutes).

- Or, in place of sharing, or to supplement the sharing, you can play one of the DVDs or CDs that goes with the week's teaching or a portion thereof.

- Lead the group in a discussion, exploring from the questions at the end of each chapter.

- Ask everyone to commit to apply the mission points for the coming week.

- Close the study with a time of prayer to seal the missions and commitments made. Give out next week's assignment, for all to read the next chapter to prepare for the upcoming class.

Congregational teaching, preaching, or classes

The Harbinger Companion With Study Guide is also made for pastors, congregations, teachers, and classes. This companion combined with the CD/DVD presentations very naturally leads to congregational prayer and revival. Here are some simple steps for leading a congregation or large class through the thirteen-week teaching.

- Pastor or teacher: Have everyone first read *The Harbinger* and obtain a copy of the study guide *(The Harbinger Companion)* so they can explore, fill in the answers, do the applications, and fully participate each week.

- Prepare a sermon series or weekly teachings based on the chapters of this companion guide.

- Or, in place of sharing, or in addition to, or to supplement the sharing, you can play the DVD or CD that goes with the week's teaching or a portion of a CD.

- Lead in prayer, consecration, and commitment (based on the life application points).

- If in a class, lead the class in a discussion, exploring from the questions at the end of each chapter.

- Ask everyone to commit to apply the mission points for the coming week.

Important note for all formats

Don't feel you have to get to all the questions that are at the end of a chapter. Some chapters have more questions (like the ones on the Nine Harbingers) and others have less. Do as much as time will allow, or choose which ones you want to focus on from the start. People can do more at another time, at home, in individual study, and so on.

We pray that this study guide will be an effective tool for equipping you to discover God's message for America and your part in bringing about repentance, restoration, and revival in our land.

■ SECTION I ■
EXPLORING THE HARBINGERS

א ת

Chapter 1

The HARBINGER:
An INTRODUCTION

The Ancient Mystery

IS IT POSSIBLE that there exists an ancient mystery that holds the secret of America's future? *The Harbinger* is the revealing of a mystery so precise that it contains the words of American leaders before they utter them, shows their actions before they take them, and pinpoints the exact dates—even hours—of the greatest collapses in Wall Street history.

The mystery of *The Harbinger* begins over twenty-seven hundred years ago in the days of ancient Israel. In the last days of that kingdom, before its judgment, there manifested Nine Harbingers, or signs, of a nation heading to judgment. But the people of Israel disregarded the signs and continued on a path of defiance against God. A number of years were given to them to either turn back to God or enter into judgment. They refused to turn back. And in 722 BC they were destroyed.

What is stunning, eerie, and even downright scary is that those same

Nine Harbingers of judgment that appeared in Israel's last days are now reappearing—*on American soil*. Some have appeared in New York City. Some have appeared in Washington DC. Some have appeared in the form of objects, others as events, even ceremonies. Some have involved the highest leaders of the land, even the president of the United States.

This ancient mystery holds the key to everything from politics, economics, culture, the course of history, the future of America, the future of every American, and that of the world.

The Word and the Story

From the day of its release *The Harbinger* has been rapidly spreading across the country. From the week of its release it has topped the Christian and secular charts. In the Christian world it has been praised and hailed by pastors, ministry leaders, and Bible school and seminary professors across denominational lines from Baptist to charismatic. It has been described as "mind-boggling," "amazing," and "stunning." It has led to Bible studies and prayer movements for repentance, salvation, and revival.

Its impact in the non-Christian and secular realms has been no less dramatic. In one state legislature every member was given a copy of the book. It has even reached Capitol Hill and been read by members of Congress.

The Harbinger was written in a period of four months. It happened at a rapid pace as if the book had already been written beforehand and was now only being copied down. The story of its publication was equally unique. (See chapter 24, "The Story Behind the Story.")

The Harbinger is, in essence, nonfiction. Its message deals with reality, fact, what has happened, what is happening, and what is yet to happen. Yet it is framed in a narrative, the story of a man who encounters a mysterious figure known as "the prophet," who reveals to him a mystery going back over twenty-five hundred years but in which is contained a secret that touches everything. The prophet gives the man nine clay seals, each seal holding a mystery that has to be deciphered, each mystery a puzzle piece in a still larger and still unfolding revelation.

The narrative is simply a vessel, a delivery system, through which the revelations are given. In the same way, narratives, images, parables, symbols, stories, and allegories are used to communicate spiritual, moral, or prophetic truth throughout the Bible. The narrative is simply the framework around the essence. The essence is the revelation—that which the prophet reveals, the ancient mystery behind what is now taking place in America.

What *The Harbinger* Is Not

Before we move to what *The Harbinger* is, it is important to clarify what *The Harbinger* is not.

Any message or book of this nature and scale is bound to be misunderstood by some and met with confusion by others. Below is a very brief list of what *The Harbinger* is not. (For more detail on this and other questions, see "Frequently Asked Questions About *The Harbinger* and Jonathan Cahn.")

The Harbinger...

- Does *not* say that Isaiah was *prophesying* of America or that the harbingers are *fulfillments* of the Scripture but rather that the biblical pattern of judgment revealed in Isaiah is now replaying in America
- Does *not* say that God made a covenant with America
- Does *not* in any way affect the interpretation or hermeneutic of Isaiah 9 as speaking of Israel
- Does *not* advocate Replacement Theology, the teaching that God is finished with Israel; the author firmly advocates the opposite, that God's promises to Israel will yet be fulfilled
- Does *not* say that God was on the side of America's enemies any more than He was on the side of Israel's enemies; He was against them
- Does *not* advocate Dominion Theology, the teaching that believers are to have dominion over the world in this age

- Is *not*, in its essence, fiction. The essence of *The Harbinger* is the communicating of truth, facts, biblical patterns, connections, mysteries, and what is happening in reality. These things are framed around and communicated in a narrative. Thus, the fictional story is a vessel to deliver truth, as in a parable.

The Impact of *The Harbinger*: Reasons Why

Perhaps the reason the message is resonating so deeply across America and around the world is because it connects the dots to bring forth a powerful revelation of something most believers have felt in their hearts— that America is on a path to judgment and God has been sending warnings and wake-up calls. *The Harbinger* reveals that this is not just a feeling but a precise biblical phenomenon that lies behind everything from 9/11 to the collapse of the American economy, taking place literally before our eyes and holding the secret of our nation's future.

The overwhelming majority of those who have read it believe that *The Harbinger* has caught on to the degree that it has because its message represents the urgent sounding of an alarm, a biblical revelation, and a prophetic warning that has been appointed to go forth for such a time as this.

What *The Harbinger* Is

The foundation of *The Harbinger*, which is very simple and centered in sound scriptural parameters, is this:

1. God is righteous and judges nations.

2. God is merciful and warns of judgment.

3. God acts in a way that is consistent with His nature and His workings as revealed in Scripture. Thus, the pattern, template, and progression of national judgment in ancient times may again be replayed.

4. God is able to warn a nation of judgment by using the Scriptures.

The Bible reveals that God's actions concerning Israel as recorded in the Hebrew Scriptures were written for our instruction. God is the same yesterday, today, and forever. The issue of judgment versus mercy is just as relevant today as it was in ancient times. In God's dealings with ancient Israel we find templates, blueprints, and patterns of judgment. One of these templates concerns the judgment of the northern kingdom. And one of the key scriptures concerning the judgment of the northern kingdom is Isaiah 9:10.

In fact, one of the most conservative and revered and classic of Bible commentaries speaks of Isaiah 9:10 and the surrounding verses as exactly this, a template and pattern of warning and judgment applicable well beyond the borders and times of ancient Israel:

> I. Its common course (of warning and judgment)
>
> 1. First comes some serious departure from God or from his service on the part of the nation....
>
> 2. Then comes the Divine correction. This may be in the form of prophetic, or parental or pastoral rebuke, or of some serious reverse in temporal affairs.... Then comes the resentment and revolt of the human will against the Divine. Instead of hearkening, heeding, and repenting, the nation... determines to act in a spirit of defiance. In its own strength, it will rise above its present circumstances... it will turn its fallen bricks into massive stones that will not fail; it will exchange its feeble sycamores that are cut down for strong cedars....[1]

Israel and America

Why should a biblical template of judgment that manifested in ancient Israel be manifesting again in twenty-first-century America? Israel is Israel. America is America. Neither one replaces the other. One can certainly go on endlessly listing the differences between the two nations. So why would the judgment pattern or warning signs given to one now appear to the other?

Why does it have to be America? It doesn't. The signs could appear in any nation in danger of judgment because (1) God is consistent and acts in consistency with His Word, and (2) these are signs of national judgment.

While it doesn't have to be America, there is a rationale for why it takes place here. God warns through calamity, but calamities, as with other circumstances, can be taken in any number of ways. For a calamity and current events to match up with a specific scripture gives clarity and specificity to the message. Thus a clear warning is given.

What nation would be most likely able to discern, understand, or hear such a warning? A nation that rests on a Judeo-Christian or biblical foundation.

Beyond this, America is uniquely paralleled to ancient Israel in many ways. From its very conception it was built upon a biblical foundation and dedicated for God's purposes, as was Israel. As we will see, it was even formed after the pattern of ancient Israel. Now, as with ancient Israel, it is falling away from that foundation. And so for the ancient pattern of judgment, once manifested in Israel, to manifest again in America, the nation patterned from its conception after that of Israel, has its own logic.

What about other nations? Haven't some nations sinned as badly as or worse than America? Absolutely. So it was with ancient Israel. But there is a principle in the Bible that says this: to those to whom much is given, much is required (Luke 12:48). Americans have been given much. We have been blessed more than the people of any nation. If we now turn away from the God of our foundation, the God of our blessings, much will be required.

What about the fact that 9/11 was carried out by evil men? The Assyrians who carried out the attack on ancient Israel were also evil men. God was not with them or for them. God was against them. So too God is against the evil of al Qaeda and other terrorist organizations. But God allows and uses all things, both good and evil, for the purposes of redemption.

God allowed ancient Israel to be shaken, not for the purpose of destruction, but for redemption, to wake up the nation, to call her back to Himself, to avoid destruction. Israel refused to wake up or to turn back and was destroyed.

America is now witnessing the same pattern of judgment, the same signs, the same progression. Will America turn back? Will there be judgment or redemption? *The Harbinger* is a wake-up call, the sounding of an alarm for the purpose of redemption, salvation, repentance, revival, and restoration. So too is the purpose of what you are about to read.

WEEK 1 EXPLORE *and* APPLY

Read chapters 1–2 of *The Harbinger*.

Read Jeremiah 33:3 and Isaiah 55:6–11.

■ *Explore* ■

God is love, and God must bring judgment against evil. How can both of these propositions be true (even at the same time)?

Israel is the only nation spoken of in the Bible with which God entered into a covenant. But would you say America is a special nation? If so, explain why.

What is the connection between America and Israel that goes back to America's own conception?

God is consistent in His ways. What does that mean concerning national judgment?

The Bible gives a record of God's dealings in history. Is what happened with God and Israel in ancient times relevant to us today? Are there principles or patterns that hold true now?

In 586 BC judgment and destruction came to the nation of Judah. Were only the wicked affected? Explain.

Does God promise believers that they won't have problems in this world? If not, then what does He promise His people?

Does God use trouble or calamity as warnings or wake-up calls to nations? How so?

What positive or redemptive purposes can come about through calamity?

Why must God judge?

Even before you knew about *The Harbinger*, did you feel that America was in danger of judgment? Why?

What do you sense is happening to America?

Do you remember a different time in America when things that are taking place now concerning morality would have been unthinkable? What about things that took place then that would now be unthinkable?

What specific things do you remember about America in the past? If you remember such things as these below, ponder or share.

- ❑ There was prayer in schools.
- ❑ Sermons on television and sermonettes closed virtually every station and broadcast day.
- ❑ There were Christmas songs or plays in school and Christmas and Easter recesses.
- ❑ Business and commerce closed down on Sunday because it was "the Lord's day."
- ❑ The name of Jesus was spoken in public gatherings.
- ❑ All men and women living together on television were married.
- ❑ Pornography was something relegated to seedy places, and not easily accessible.
- ❑ Living together was considered a sin.
- ❑ The killing of the unborn was universally seen as immoral.
- ❑ Divorce was uncommon.
- ❑ The idea that marriage could be redefined was unthinkable.
- ❑ The idea that images of God and Jesus could be used in comedy and mockery was unthinkable.
- ❑ America was the number one creditor nation in the world, and there was little thought of a day when its global preeminence could come to an end.

Isaiah 9 is written to and about Israel. But does God use His Word, and words given to Israel in ancient times, to speak to us beyond ancient times and beyond the borders of Israel? Explain.

Does God send warnings before He judges?

What patterns of national judgment can you identify from the Bible?

Can you cite places in the Bible where He does this very thing?

What different ways does God communicate to His people or to a nation today?

In what direction do you feel America is heading? Why is this significant?

If America continues on its present course, what do you believe it will be like in ten years? Twenty years?

What do you believe God is saying to America?

What is the hope?

■ *Spiritual Truth* ■

Look again at Jeremiah 33:3 and Isaiah 55:6–11. What are these passages saying?

If these things are the case, why is it a mistake for believers to be closed or to think we know all there is to know about God and His Word?

What then should be the attitude of our hearts and minds?

■ *Mission to Apply This Week* ■

As we begin this course, open your heart and mind to hear the calling and voice of God. Ask God to show you what He wants you to know and what He wants you to do, what He wants for your life.

Commit this week to opening your heart and mind to be able to actually listen to God, to hear from Him, even things you may never have heard before.

Pray, asking Him to lead you as never before and seek to follow His voice. (For groups, take time to allow everyone to pray individually before the leader closes by asking God to seal the prayers prayed.)

Write down your mission for the week in the space below.

Prepare for next week (groups only): This week read, go over, and explore the next chapter, "Ancient Israel: The Rise and the Apostasy."

■ *Write Down* ■

1. Your thoughts, notes, and insights

2. What you believe the Lord is calling you to do

3. Your mission for the days ahead

Chapter 2

ANCIENT ISRAEL:
The RISE *and the* APOSTASY

HOW DOES A nation that once knew God become a stranger to Him and even find itself at war against Him? How does it forget the godly foundations on which it was conceived? How does an individual who once knew God fall away from Him? In this study we will open up the pattern, the progression, the dynamics, and the transformation that changed ancient Israel from a nation that served God to one that warred against Him.

The Mystery Begins: Ancient Israel

The mystery of *The Harbinger* begins with ancient Israel. Nearly four millennia ago Israel was conceived through a promise. God called Abraham to leave Mesopotamia for Canaan where He vowed to bless Abraham and make his descendants a great nation in whom "all the families of the earth shall be blessed" (Gen. 12:3). The Lord repeated this promise to Isaac, Jacob, and Jacob's twelve sons, who were the fathers of Israel's twelve tribes.

Along with the privilege of being God's people and dwelling in His Promised Land came a sacred call to be "a kingdom of priests and a holy nation" (Exod. 19:6), a light to the nations by obeying His Torah. The Law exhorted His people to remember their God, who had freed them from slavery in Egypt. It instructed them to trust and worship Him alone. It commanded them to magnify His name, to enter into His rest, to honor and protect human life, to cherish sexual purity and the sanctity of marriage, to live with honesty and integrity, to be thankful for their blessings, and to love their neighbors as themselves (Exod. 20:1–17; Lev. 19:18). Obedience would bring untold honor and favor; disobedience would lead to calamity, from famine and pestilence to conquest by enemies and exile from the land (Lev. 26; Deut. 28).

When Israel walked with God, its people enjoyed great blessing and protection. During the reigns of King David and King Solomon, Israel's foes were defeated, and the nation experienced tremendous abundance and fame.

The Ancient Apostasy

Yet even Solomon in the end began to imitate the surrounding Canaanite culture, building high places for Chemosh, the god of the Moabites, and Molech, the god of the Ammonites (1 Kings 11:7).

The Lord judged Solomon by splitting Israel into two kingdoms after his death—the northern kingdom of Israel, which included ten of the twelve tribes, and the southern kingdom of Judah, including Jerusalem and the Temple.

The northern kingdom is the setting for *The Harbinger*. The year was 732 BC, nearly two hundred years after Solomon's death. Instead of building on its godly foundation, Israel had departed from it. Instead of sacrificing to the faithful God of their forefathers in His holy Temple, Israelites now sacrificed to cruel, capricious, counterfeit gods in unholy places. Instead of the Law being king, Israel's kings became the law, and lawlessness ruled the land. Instead of being a light to the nations, Israel pursued their dark ways, forsaking its God.

Apostasy

What were the ways of the peoples surrounding Israel?

Excavations...have uncovered...objects connected with sorcery, fertility cults, demon exorcism, and pagan superstitions that at times propagated themselves in Israel to such an extent that legislators, prophets, and some rulers had frequently to warn the people against them.[1]

Excavations in Palestine have uncovered...remains of infant skeletons in cemeteries around heathen altars, pointing to...widespread...[human sacrifice].[2]

[Canaanite worship]...was pornographic....It suggested that anything was permissible, promiscuity, murder, or anything else, in order to guarantee a good...harvest. It ignored the highest values...love, loyalty, purity, peace, and security—[deeming] all these things...inferior to material prosperity, physical satisfaction, and human pleasure.[3]

Canaanite deities ranged from their chief god Baal to Molech, a god represented by a hollow image above a fire into which parents would hurl their children, to Anat, a goddess of sexuality and violence, depicted as wearing a belt of heads and hands of human beings.

The Calls, the Warnings, and the End

God in His mercy sent the prophets Elijah, Elisha, Hosea, and Amos to bring Israel to her senses. Rejecting calls for repentance, their fellow Israelites persecuted them, branding them as enemies and apostates. Tolerating every god and goddess of the Middle East, Israel found the very utterance of the name of the God of Israel intolerable.

In 732 BC God sent a final warning by temporarily removing Israel's hedge of protection, permitting a limited invasion by Assyria.

Unfortunately Israel failed to heed this call to return and in 722 BC was destroyed.

> And the king of Assyria uncovered a conspiracy by Hoshea [the king of Israel]; for he had sent messengers to So, king of Egypt, and brought no tribute to the king of Assyria.... Therefore the

king of Assyria…bound him in prison.…In the ninth year of Hoshea, the king of Assyria….carried Israel away to Assyria.

—2 KINGS 17:4, 6

For so it was that the children of Israel had sinned against the LORD their God, who had brought them up out of…Egypt…and they had feared other gods, and had walked in the statutes of the nations whom the LORD had cast out from before the children of Israel.…Yet the Lord [said]…by all of His prophets…"Turn from your evil ways, and keep My commandments…which I commanded your fathers.…" Nevertheless they would not hear…they…became idolaters.…And they caused their sons and daughters to pass through the fire, practiced witchcraft and soothsaying, and sold themselves to do evil.…Therefore the LORD…removed them [Israel] from His sight.…So Israel was carried away from their own land to Assyria.

—2 KINGS 17:7–23

The Steps of Israel's Apostasy

Created to be a light to the nations, Israel became an imitator of the nations and was exiled to the nations. How did this happen?

The apostasy of a nation is similar to that of an individual. Israel's love and passion for God grew cold. Instead of rejoicing in and pursuing God, the people began pursuing and rejoicing in other things: comfort, security, gain, power, and pleasures. As the nation's love for God dissipated, other gods and idols were brought in to fill the void.

In the beginning of this apostasy Israel joined the worship of other gods to the worship of God. But in time the transformation was complete, as the nation's spiritual confusion turned into outright enmity and war against God and His ways.

By the time of her end Israel was hardly distinguishable from the pagan nations that surrounded her—except for one thing: Israel had not merely become a pagan nation, but a nation at war against the very foundation on which she was conceived, a nation in apostasy, a nation in spiritual schizophrenia against her own purpose and calling.

An Alien Nation

Israel had driven God out of its government, out of its culture, out of its national life. Israel had disregarded the Torah, the laws, the precepts, and ways of God. It had replaced the Lord with idols and worshipped and served the gods of other nations. It had descended into sexual immorality. It called good "evil" and evil "good." Israel had offered up its children as sacrifices. It had persecuted the people of God, those who still held true to His ways. And now, as the Lord sent His warnings, Israel rejected them. It had become a stranger to God, even an enemy. And in rejecting His calling to save it, Israel would have no future but destruction.

The Heart of the Matter

What was the heart of this dramatic fall? It may be found in Ezekiel 16. Ancient Jerusalem is portrayed as a woman God had adorned with beauty and splendor, but she had become a harlot to her pagan neighbors, worshipping their gods and sacrificing her children to them.

Verse 15 says: "But you trusted in your own beauty..."

Note the irony. When God blessed His people, they gloried in the blessings rather than in the One who blessed them, turning the blessings into potential curses that threatened the nation.

Put another way, God's people forgot God's love for them. "Forgetfulness of God's love is the source of all sins. Israel forgot her deliverance by God in the infancy of her national life."[4]

What was true for Israel is true for us. If we forget God's love that drew us to Him, we begin a downward spiritual and moral spiral, leading us to places we would never have chosen when we were walking with Him. If we trust in our own strengths, the very strengths He gave us, rather than in Him, they will fail us. Most importantly, a strong and loving God will seek our return, as He did with Israel, first with warnings and finally by removing hedges of protection in our lives.

God's love for us, as for His people Israel, remains unconditional. If we turn from Him, in His love He will call us and remove anything that would keep us or lead us away, even the hedge that surrounds our blessings.

WEEK 2 EXPLORE *and* APPLY

Read chapter 3 of *The Harbinger.*

Read Genesis 12:3; Exodus 19:6; Leviticus 26; Deuteronomy 28; 2 Kings 17:5–23.

▦ *Explore* ▦

What made Israel unique among the nations?

How many things can you find about the foundation and establishment of Israel that were unique among the nations?

What was God's will and calling for Israel?

How do you think a nation that was given so much at her foundation could fall away from knowing God and His ways?

How could Israel's people have forgotten Him?

Why, what was it, that you think caused them to fall away?

Do you think it happened all at once or gradually? Why?

What significance does going after many gods and personal idols hold with regard to morality? Self-centeredness? Materialism? Sensuality? And why?

In what ways did Israel become just like the nations that surrounded it—a pagan nation?

The pagan nations had never known God. So can you think of any ways that Israel must have been a nation divided against itself, against its own foundations?

Why do you think the people of Israel ended up persecuting the righteous, those who remained faithful to God and His ways (like Elijah?) What was behind the persecution?

Why do you think most people in Israel refused to listen when God called them to turn back through the prophets?

What challenges did the righteous who lived in Israel in its days of apostasy have to deal with?

How do you think they dealt with it?

■ *Spiritual Truths* ■

What spiritual and practical truths can you find in the example of Israel once knowing God and His ways and then falling away?

How can these same truths be applied not just to a nation but also to an individual?

Based on these truths, what counsel, safeguard, hedges, and advice would you give to someone to help them never fall away from God?

■ *Mission to Apply This Week* ■

What steps (try to think of three) can you take this week and put into application in your life? Make this your mission for the week and write it down in the space on the following page.

Take time now to commit this to God and pray for His help and anointing.

Seal this commitment in prayer (individually, in small groups, as a class, or congregationally).

Prepare for next week (groups only): This week read, go over, and explore the next chapter, "America's Rise and Fall."

▨ *Write Down* ▨

1. Your thoughts, notes, and insights

2. What you believe the Lord is calling you to do

3. Your mission for the days ahead

Chapter 3

AMERICA'S RISE *and* FALL

The City on a Hill

T HE BIBLE SAYS that "righteousness exalts a nation, but sin is a reproach to any people" (Prov. 14:34). We have seen how an ancient nation turned from righteousness to sin, from worshipping God to warring against Him. We now turn to a modern nation—America—one that was also founded on God's Word for His glory. While America has not replaced ancient Israel, America was established after the pattern of ancient Israel and has followed in Israel's apostasy from God. In this study we explore how this transformation happened and how it followed the dynamics of the ancient apostasy.

America's spiritual foundation was laid by godly men and women, beginning with the Pilgrims and Puritans who left Europe in order to practice their biblical faith freely. Starting with the Mayflower Compact in 1620 and continuing with the chartering of the Massachusetts Bay Colony, they labored to build a new civilization on biblical principles, dedicated to God's purposes, a "city upon a hill," in the words of Puritan leader John Winthrop.[1]

And as America's forerunners embraced the God of the Bible, so too did they identify with the people of the Bible and the covenant at Sinai.

21

After the Pattern of Israel

[They] believed their own lives [were] a literal reenactment of the Biblical drama of the Hebrew nation. They [saw themselves] as the children of Israel; America was their Promised Land...the pact of...Plymouth Rock was God's...Covenant; [they] saw themselves as...a people chosen to build their new commonwealth in the Covenant entered into at Sinai.[2]

The Pilgrims' celebration of Thanksgiving came from the Old Testament Feast of Tabernacles or *Sukkot*.[3] The earliest legislation of the New England colonies was influenced by the Hebrew Scriptures. America's first colleges, such as Harvard, Yale, and Princeton, were established to train ministers of God's Word.[4] Hebrew words or phrases often accompanied their emblems or seals. More than a century later, when the first design of the official seal of the United States was proposed, the motto around the seal read, "Rebellion to tyrants is obedience to God." The seal depicts the Jews crossing the Red Sea.[5]

The Nation and Its Rock

This motto acknowledged God as America's ultimate king. God ruled through His law, with no earthly king above the law any more than he was above God. This argument against tyranny led to the Declaration of Independence, the Revolutionary War, and a brand-new republic enjoying the blessings of liberty.

Examining fifteen thousand pieces of late-eighteenth-century American political literature, Donald Lutz found that the Bible was cited far more often than any other writing. America's founders referenced it more than all Enlightenment authors combined.[6] In the nineteenth century, Andrew Jackson called the Word of God "the rock on which our Republic rests."[7] Abraham Lincoln made numerous positive references to God and the Bible throughout his presidency and spoke of the judgment of God upon the nation. In the twentieth century, President Harry Truman noted, "The fundamental basis for this nation's laws was given to Moses on the Mount."[8]

The Head of Nations

As the Scriptures proclaim, "Blessed is the nation whose God is the LORD" (Ps. 33:12). American history is impossible to understand without understanding its founding vision to be a city on a hill and a light to the nations. And as America sought to fulfill this vision, it was blessed more than any other nation in the modern world. By the end of the eighteenth century it had won independence from the world's greatest military power and ratified its Constitution. By the close of the nineteenth century the United States spanned an entire continent, from the Atlantic to the Pacific. In the twentieth century the United States became the world's most powerful nation, both economically and militarily.

America blessed the world by sending out more missionaries, bringing in more refugees, producing more food and other essentials, creating more technological marvels, and defeating more tyrants—fascist and communist alike—than any country in history. And as America blessed the Jewish people by providing them refuge and the new state of Israel with recognition and support, God honored His pledge in Genesis 12:3 to bless those who bless His people.

The nation and its people were never without sin. But spiritual revivals kept bringing America back to God and His Word. Its first major revival was in the 1740s and led not only to the American Revolution but also to more revivals lasting well into the nineteenth century, birthing major reform movements like the drive to abolish slavery.

The Fall

From the days of the Puritans onward, America's forerunners had warned what would happen if America turned firmly from her foundations by turning against God. About 170 years later, John Adams warned, "Our Constitution was made only for a moral and religious people. It is wholly inadequate to the government of any other."[9]

Yet despite these warnings, America repeated the pattern of Israel's ancient northern kingdom and experienced an equally dramatic moral and spiritual decline. The seeds were sown nearly a century ago, as the leaders of America's historic churches began to embrace radical skepticism and doubt the Bible as God's Word. These seeds grew into a belief that "religion" was a private subjective matter, not an objective public concern. In 1963 the US Supreme Court decided to ban public school prayer, the first of a series of major steps taken to drive God out of the nation's public life.

As respect for God's Word and ways declined, so did America's culture. The assault on the American family began with rising divorce rates and continued with skyrocketing out-of-wedlock births and finally the drive to redefine marriage, family, and sin itself. Across society the desire for ceaseless entertainment and instant gratification overrode self-discipline and values, fueling an explosion in pornography, sexual promiscuity, and drug addiction, along with the revival of pagan occult practices under the banner of New Age movements.

In 1973 the Supreme Court decreed "abortion on demand" to be the law of the land. As Israel sacrificed thousands of its children on the altars of Baal and Molech, so now America sacrifices millions of unborn on the altar of personal choice. Christians and others who protest this rising tide of apostasy are increasingly mocked, ridiculed, marginal-ized, and ostracized. As Israel had done thousands of years earlier, now America does. It calls good "evil" and evil "good."

What happened to ancient Israel is now happening in America. Our nation has forgotten its godly beginnings, trusting in God's blessings rather than the God of all blessings.

John Witherspoon, a signer of the Declaration of Independence, had warned precisely against this temptation with these words, "While we give praise to God...for His interposition on our behalf, let us guard against...trusting in, or boasting of, an arm of flesh."[10]

As America patterned itself after Israel in its conception, so now it follows the pattern of Israel's fall. Today, Israel's ancient northern kingdom is but a footnote of history. Without revival and restoration, America risks a similar fate.

WEEK 3 EXPLORE *and* APPLY

Reread chapter 3 of *The Harbinger.*

Listen to or watch the accompanying resource, *The City on the Hill* CD or DVD.

Read Proverbs 14:34; Psalm 33:12; Psalm 127:1; and 2 Kings 17:5–23.

▩ *Explore* ▩

How many parallels can you find between the founding of America and the founding of Israel?

Why do you think these parallels exist?

What importance did ancient Israel hold for the Puritans in establishing American society?

How central was the name of Jesus and the cause of the gospel in America's founding?

How many examples can you find to show this?

For what reason was the American school system established?

For what reasons were universities like Harvard established?

How has America's biblical origins and Judeo-Christian foundations made America unique?

In what ways has America fulfilled its founding vision to be a light to the world and a vessel for good?

In what specific ways has America followed the ways of God?

In what ways has God blessed America?

Look at the notes, findings, and insights you found in the study on Israel's apostasy and fall. (See also 2 Kings 17.) How many parallels can you find between Israel's departure from God and what has happened and is happening now in America, especially in the realms of:

❑ Spiritual complacency

❑ Materialism

❑   Forgetting its foundation and consecration to God

❑   Departing from and adulterating the Word of God

❑   Progressively ruling God out of its life (government, culture, etc.)

❑   No longer passing on the knowledge of God to its children

❑   Worshipping and serving other gods and idols

❑   Falling into and celebrating sexual immorality

❑   Declaring good "evil" and evil "good"—Right "wrong" and wrong "right"

❑   Increasingly warring against the ways of God

❑   Offering up its children

❑   Persecuting the people who remain faithful to God's ways

Why do you think this is happening?

▨ *Spiritual Truths* ▨

Looking at the example of America's falling away from the ways of God, what spiritual and practical truths can you find?

How can these same truths be applied to an individual?

Based now on the case of America, what truths, counsel, safeguards, and hedges can you give, and how can you apply this to your own life?

▨ *Mission to Apply This Week* ▨

What parts of this falling away in American culture are you most vulnerable to partake of or be influenced by? (Answers might include materialism, sexual immorality, complacency, idolatry, the love of money, self-centeredness, etc.)

What specific steps can you take this week to repent of this, to overcome, to stay farther away, or to take steps to go in the opposite direction? Make this your mission for this week and write it in the space below.

Take time now to commit this to God and pray for His help and anointing.

Seal this commitment in prayer (individually, in small groups, as a class, or congregationally).

Prepare for next week (groups only): This week read, go over, and explore the next chapter, "The Harbingers: The Breach to the Gazit Stone."

■ *Write Down* ■

1. Your thoughts, notes, and insights

2. What you believe the Lord is calling you to do

3. Your mission for the days ahead

Chapter 4

The HARBINGERS:
The BREACH *to the* GAZIT STONE

Warning Signs of Judgment

HOW DOES GOD warn a nation of judgment? Are there patterns revealed in the Bible? How does God warn and call us? How is an ancient pattern and template of judgment and warning actually manifested on American soil? In this study we explore what happens when a nation grows deaf to the call of God and how the warnings of judgment must become severer in their pattern and progression. In this chapter we'll cover the pattern from Isaiah 9:10, which includes the manifestation of the Breach, the Terrorist, the Bricks, the Tower, and the Gazit Stone.

The First Harbinger:
The Breach

The breaching of ancient Israel

God's covenant with Israel included the promise of protection from threats to its safety, security, and existence.

> I will give peace in the land, and you shall lie down, and none will make you afraid. I will rid the land of evil beasts, and the sword will not go through your land. You will chase your enemies, and they shall fall by the sword before you.
>
> —LEVITICUS 26:6–7

This hedge of protection, however, came with a condition—namely, obedience to God's will.

> If you walk in My statutes and keep My commandments, and perform them…
>
> —LEVITICUS 26:3

When Israel began to turn against the Lord and His commands, His Word itself provided numerous warnings of what would befall the nation, from disease and famine to invasion by enemies and ultimately exile from the land. (See Leviticus 26:14–39; Deuteronomy 28:15–68.)

When these words of warning, delivered hundreds of years earlier through Moses, were ignored, God sent messengers to call the people and their leaders back to Him. In response to the sins of the northern kingdom, He sent prophets like Elijah, Elisha, Hosea, and Amos. Responding to the trespasses of Judah, He sent prophets like Isaiah and Jeremiah with the same message of warning and repentance.

It was only when the words of both Moses and the prophets fell on deaf ears—when there was no other recourse—that God began to move against the nation's hedge of protection:

> I will take away its hedge, and it shall be burned; and break down
> its wall, and it shall be trampled down.
>
> —ISAIAH 5:5

Yet God in His mercy did not completely destroy ancient Israel's hedge at first. Instead He allowed a breach in Israel's defenses, a temporary invasion by its enemies.

In 732 BC God permitted Tiglath-Pileser III, the king of Assyria, to sack the northern kingdom of Israel. This was a warning, a wake-up call, a foreshadowing on a small and limited scale of the destruction that would befall the nation years later if it did not turn back. The same pattern can be seen in the fall and destruction of the southern kingdom of Judah. In 605 BC God let the Babylonians, commanded by Nebuchadnezzar, invade the borders of Judah. In neither case did He allow either kingdom to fall. But in both instances it was a final warning and wake-up call to return to God.

The breaching of America

Wally Gobetz

To a remarkable extent America has enjoyed a similar hedge of protection as ancient Israel did. And just as God sent prophets to Israel to turn it from sin, anointed preachers have risen in America to help bring revival throughout our nation's history. But from the mid-twentieth century onward, America's spiritual and moral decline progressed at a pace unprecedented in her history.

By the late twentieth century, with prayer removed from the nation's public schools, expressions of faith increasingly banned from the public square, and revivals less frequent or powerful, America had sunk even further into moral and spiritual decline. Christians who tried to call the nation back to God were mocked and ridiculed.

On September 11, 2001, America's hedge of protection was breached. Though many were afraid to say so, across the land many saw it as a wake-up call. There was even an instinctive response throughout the nation to flock to houses of worship. It was the shadow of a revival that almost came but never did.

Without repentance, without a change of course, there can be no revival or hope. And in the months and years after 9/11, America largely returned to business as usual.

The Second Harbinger: The Terrorist

The ancient terrorist

In dealing with the sins of the northern kingdom of Israel, the instrument that God allowed to breach its hedge of protection was the nation of Assyria. By the time the breach occurred, in 732 BC, the Assyrians had conquered much of the Middle East. They deployed a huge standing army and new means of warfare such as the movable tower, the battering ram, and wall breakers. They struck fear into the hearts of peoples across the region through the calculated use of terror, the earliest example of organized psychological warfare.

After conquering a city, the Assyrians would burn it to the ground and commit public atrocities of every kind to discourage rebellion against their rule. One of their kings, Ashurnasirpal II, even boasted: "I built a pillar...against his city gate and I flayed all the chiefs who had revolted and I covered the pillar with their skin. Some I walled up within the pillar, some I impaled upon the pillar on stakes...and I cut off the limbs of the...royal officers who had rebelled."[1]

The terrorists of 9/11

Not only spiritually but also literally, the terrorists who breached America's defenses on September 11, 2001, are related to the ancient Assyrians who breached ancient Israel's divine hedge. Both were Middle Eastern, Semitic people. Arabic, the language these twenty-first-century terrorists spoke and in which they carried out their attack is the sister language of the Assyrians, Akkadian, in which the attack of ancient Israel in Isaiah 9:10 was carried out.

And just as the Assyrian invasion of 732 BC would draw ancient Israel into military conflict, so too did al Qaeda's attack on 9/11 draw America into war, eventually in Iraq, the very land of ancient Assyria, including the city of Mosul, within which were the ruins of Nineveh, the ancient capital of Assyria.

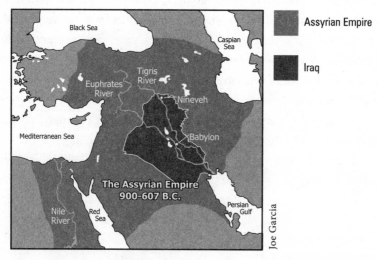

The Key:
The Vow of Isaiah 9:10

So how did ancient Israel respond to the breach in her hedge of protection by Assyria's incursion? The answer is recorded in Isaiah 9:10:

> The bricks have fallen, but we will rebuild with hewn stone; the sycamores have been cut down, but we will plant cedars in their place.[2]
>
> —Author's translation

Simply stated, ancient Israel vowed to rebuild rather than recognizing the destruction inflicted by Assyria as God's final warning to repent.

In Isaiah 9:9 God condemned this attitude as a sign of "pride and arrogance of heart." While there was nothing wrong with a desire to rebuild after an attack, there was plenty wrong with Israel's refusal to search its ways, its "self-confident unwillingness to see the judgments of God,"[3] its determination to silence God's alarm, and its ignoring of His call to turn from its ways and trust Him again. The nation was vowing to continue on its course without God and against God—and to do so more strongly than ever before.

Clearly the words of Isaiah 9:10 pertain to ancient Israel. But what if that same message or warning of judgment could be manifested elsewhere, to another nation that once knew God and had fallen away? Those words would become a harbinger of that country's future, a sign that it is in danger of judgment and has now been given a warning and a call to return.

As *The Harbinger* illustrates, the same Nine Harbingers or signs of warning that appeared in ancient Israel before her destruction have now reappeared in America. Isaiah 9:10 is the key to all of them, unlocking each of their mysteries and joining them all together. Each of them is connected and, when joined to the other eight, forms an unmistakable prophetic message of divine warning before judgment.

The fallen bricks of ancient Israel

The breach and the terrorist are the first two harbingers and the context for the other seven. As we have seen, both of these harbingers reappeared in America on 9/11.

The Third Harbinger is found in the opening words of Isaiah 9:10: "The bricks have fallen." These words state the obvious: Assyria had attacked Israel and wrought physical damage, as evidenced by heaps of fallen brick from collapsed structures.

But this leads us to questions arising from the first two harbingers: Why did God allow the breach in the first place? Why did He let the forces of Assyrian terror enter? Why was Israel's hedge of protection removed, leaving it defenseless and leading to the damage that was now plainly visible through piles of bricks appearing where buildings once stood?

Seen in this way, the fallen bricks highlight the progression of God's many warnings to the nation, first through the ancient choice of blessings or curses laid before Israel by Moses in Leviticus and Deuteronomy, next through the contemporary warnings uttered by Israel's prophets, and finally through the breach in Israel's defenses and the terrorist forces entering the land. It demanded from the people and their leaders an unequivocal response of repentance.

The fallen bricks of America

Photo by Bri Rodriguez/FEMA

Has this Third Harbinger, like the first two, been manifested in America?

The answer is yes.

In the aftermath of the 9/11 attacks, there was no more visible or identifiable sign of what had happened than the surreal, haunting image at Ground Zero, several stories high, containing heaps of brick, all that was left of the twin towers of downtown Manhattan, the financial capital of the world and symbol of America's unmatched economic and financial strength and dominance.

As with ancient Israel, the fallen bricks bear witness not only to literal damage but also to the first two harbingers of the breach and the terrorist, proclaiming a stark warning to a nation that had left its godly foundations and had resisted every prior entreaty to turn back to God.

As with Israel, the damage was limited; the judgment was not final. As with Israel, it was visible to all; a call to repentance was being made. As with Israel, America chose to reject the call and move on.

The Fourth Harbinger: The Tower

The tower of ancient Israel

Taken together, the first three harbingers—the breach, the terrorist, and the bricks—tell the story of a nation that abandons its godly roots, leading to God's removing His hedge of protection and blessing when all other warnings fail, resulting in a sudden but limited attack from a fierce enemy, triggering a vow to rebuild but not repent:

The bricks have fallen, but we will rebuild...

The Fourth Harbinger reveals a nation that not only neglects to repent but also openly embraces a spirit of defiance.

The bricks have fallen, but we will rebuild *with hewn stone.*

—ISAIAH 9:10

How is this defiance? The fallen bricks were made of clay and straw, but ancient Israel vowed to replace this material with something much stronger: hewn stone. It was a vow to come out of the attack stronger than before. Missing was even a hint of critical introspection leading to a change of heart toward God. Any new construction, therefore, would represent the nation's defiance of God's call.

A number of commentaries highlight the defiance shown through ancient Israel's words.

> It is the defiance of a people who, far from being repentant, glory in their iniquity.[4]

> To be heedless when God is speaking...is iniquitous enough, but to act in deliberate defiance...is, by many degrees, worse.[5]

The American tower

Has this Fourth Harbinger, like the previous three, reappeared in America? It has.

In the days, months, and years after 9/11, three of the words from Isaiah 9:10, uttered by ancient Israel in response to the damage incurred by the Assyrian attack, were uttered repeatedly by American leaders—from governors to mayors to the president of the United States—in reply to the al Qaeda attack: "We will rebuild."

Moreover, in virtually all of the speeches delivered on the subject by these leaders, they spoke of America's determination to build bigger, better, and stronger than ever.

In addition, in many of the speeches uttered after 9/11, the word *defiance* was used in relation to the rebuilding. One example, from a senior US senator, is as follows:

> [W]e should…rebuild the towers of the World Trade Center and show the world we are not afraid. We are defiant.[6]

Finally, in the aftermath of 9/11, America settled upon the building of a structure at Ground Zero that would fully represent its aspirations in the rebuilding effort. It was the Freedom Tower.

From the tower of Babel in Genesis onward, towers in the Scriptures can represent the elevation of human pride over a spirit of humility and obedience to God. Moreover, an alternative rendering of Isaiah 9:10, coming from the Septuagint, a Greek translation of the Hebrew Scripture more than twenty centuries ago, is as follows:

> The bricks have fallen down…but come…let us build for ourselves *a tower.*

Just as ancient Israel did, in the wake of the calamity America embarks on a campaign of rebuilding, to rebuild stronger than before on the ground of its fallen bricks. A tower rises from the ruins, a symbol of defiance.

The Fifth Harbinger:
The Gazit Stone

The Gazit Stone of Israel

The first part of Israel's vow ends with the words *hewn stone*. In this lies the Fifth Harbinger. In the original Hebrew of the passage, the word is *gazit*. Besides "hewn stone," it may also be translated as a carved or quarried stone, a stone quarried, chiseled, and carved out of mountain rock.

After the Assyrian attack of 732 BC, following the vow to rebuild, the people of Israel would go to the mountains and quarries to carve, shape, and smooth the Gazit Stone and bring it back to where the bricks had fallen and begin the rebuilding.

The significance of the *Gazit Stone* and the act of putting it in place of the fallen bricks has to do with the difference in the two objects. Clay brick was brittle, flimsy, weak, and easily destroyed, but hewn stone was not. It was thus a symbol of strength—and not only of strength but of greatness. With hewn stone the nation could build not only stronger than before but also bigger and higher. Again, it was not about restoration but defiance. For Israel, the Gazit Stone symbolized the nation's hope of rebuilding itself stronger and greater than before. But in reality, it was the embodiment of their defiance and rejection of God's calling.

The American Gazit Stone

AP Images / Dean Cox

Has this Fifth Harbinger—national defiance in the form of a stone—appeared in America like the prior four harbingers? Yes.

The first act of America's rebuilding was to cut out of a mountain in upstate New York a massive rectangular block of stone, a biblical *Gazit Stone*. The second act was to bring this stone to the ground where America's bricks had fallen: Ground Zero. As America's Gazit Stone was laid on the pavement where calamity had struck, American leaders gathered around it in a ceremony of dedication. In this ceremony the leaders spoke multiple vows of defiance over the quarried stone, making it into a symbol of American resurgence. One of those leaders unwittingly used the same exact phrase used in commentaries on Isaiah 9:10 to describe the fatal mistake of Israel's leaders:

> Today, we, the heirs of that revolutionary *spirit of defiance*, lay this cornerstone...[7]

WEEK 4 EXPLORE *and* APPLY

Read chapters 4–9 of *The Harbinger.*

Watch or listen to the accompanying resource, *"The Harbinger* I*"* DVD or CD (from *The Harbinger: The Full Revelation* eight-disc album).

Read Isaiah 9:8–10; Leviticus 26:1–39; Deuteronomy 28:15–68.

▧ *Explore* ▧

The Breach

In 732 BC the Assyrians invaded Israel and then withdrew. About ten years later they returned, and Israel was destroyed. In 605 BC the Babylonians first invaded Judah. Years later they returned, and Judah was destroyed. What pattern can you see in this? What purpose could this pattern serve?

God gave Israel a promise that if the nation followed Him, it would be kept safe. For a long period of time the northern kingdom of Israel was kept safe. Do you think the people realized that it was God's grace that was keeping them safe? Why or why not?

When the Assyrians first invaded the land, what message was God sending to Israel?

America has long been kept safe from enemy attacks. Do you think most Americans clearly see this as God's grace, or do they take it for granted? Have Americans in the past had a sense of invincibility?

What made 9/11 unique in American history?

America has been the strongest superpower on the earth and protected by the most sophisticated defense system in the world. And yet all of its sophisticated systems failed on 9/11. What truth can you find in that?

The Terrorist

The Assyrians were among the most evil and ruthless people in world history yet God used them for His purposes. What truths can we find in that?

Was God siding with the Assyrians?

How do we know He was not?

Can God use evil people and evil kingdoms? How so? Where in the Bible can you find examples of this principle?

After 9/11 believers across the nation sensed it was a wake-up call to America from God. Yet many were afraid to say this? Why?

What is God's promise concerning how all things—including bad circumstances—work for believers?

The Bricks

What kind of bricks did the Israelites use to build their buildings? Why were these building materials relatively weak?

What larger message of national warning might there be in the images of fallen buildings, destruction, towers collapsing to their foundations, and heaps of ruin?

Modern buildings aren't made of clay bricks, so how might ancient Israel's destruction and national warning of judgment be translated and manifest in the modern world?

The towers of the World Trade Center were symbols of American power, preeminence, and prosperity. What could the collapse of such symbols foreshadow?

Isaiah 9:10

In the wake of the Assyrian attack in 732 BC, the people of Israel responded with the vow of Isaiah 9:10, of bricks and stones, sycamores and cedars. But what was the spiritual meaning and message of those words?

If you had to paraphrase in modern English what they were saying to God and man, what were they saying?

Rebuilding would be expected, but what is it about the vow that made it defiant of God?

What was missing from what they said?

Where in this section of Scripture does it reveal to the hearer that these words were spoken in an ungodly spirit?

In view of the fact that the Assyrian invasion was a warning, why was Israel's vow all the more ominous?

What were they choosing not to consider or realize about what had happened?

What did they trust instead of God?

In the wake of 9/11, America sought to undo the calamity by vowing to become stronger militarily, politically, and economically, to rebuild herself stronger than before. How does this parallel the fateful mistake of ancient Israel?

The Tower

The people of the northern kingdom didn't vow to rebuild with clay bricks but with hewn stone. Why is this different from restoration?

Why would quarried stones allow them to build higher buildings than before?

The oldest translation of the Bible, the Septuagint, which is quoted in the New Testament, translates Isaiah 9:10 as, "The bricks have fallen down, but come...let us build for ourselves a tower."[8] This refers to the Tower of Babel. Why do you think they did that?

What similarities can you see between the building of the tower of Babel in Genesis 11 and the building of the Israelites in Isaiah 9:10?

What was the role of towers in the ancient city and nation? What did towers represent?

Putting this all together, what significance can be found in the fact that America began building a tower at Ground Zero to symbolize its defiance in the wake of 9/11?

After 9/11 do you remember any national leader calling for repentance or a return to God?

What significance can be found in the fact that after 9/11, American leaders called continually for the nation to rebuild—and to rebuild bigger and stronger than before?

The Gazit Stone

The stone in Isaiah 9:10 is different from clay bricks in that the Hebrew word behind it, *gazit,* refers to a carved, chiseled, quarried, massive rectangular block of stone. Could these and other physical characteristics of a rock symbolize bad qualities? In what way?

After 9/11, a Gazit Stone was laid on the pavement of Ground Zero, with American leaders gathered around it in a ceremony, proclaiming vows of national defiance over it. In how many ways did what took place at Ground Zero replay and reenact what happened in Israel's last days?

What was missing from the proclamations made by American leaders that day?

Many commentaries on Isaiah 9:10 identify or allude to the nation's "spirit of defiance." In the ceremony around the stone, one of the American leaders spoke of America's "spirit of defiance." He was alluding to America's birth. But when is a "spirit of defiance" a very bad thing? In what ways can we truthfully speak of America having a "spirit of defiance" as Israel did?

▨ Spiritual Truths ▨

What was God trying to tell Israel in all this? Why did the people not hear it?

What do you believe God is trying to tell America? Why has our nation not heard it?

What do you believe God is trying to say to you now? Are you hearing it?

▨ Mission to Apply This Week ▨

In the space provided, write down what you believe God is trying to say to you right now in your life and what actions or changes you can make this week to begin responding to it. Make this your mission for the week.

Take time now to commit this to God and pray for His help and anointing.

Seal this commitment in prayer (individually, in small groups, as a class, or congregationally).

Prepare for next week (groups only): This week read, go over, and explore the next chapter, "The Harbingers; The Sycamore to the Prophecy."

■ *Write Down* ■

1. Your thoughts, notes, and insights

2. What you believe the Lord is calling you to do

3. Your mission for the days ahead

Chapter 5

The HARBINGERS:
The SYCAMORE *to the* PROPHECY

The Second Stream

THE HARBINGERS CONTINUE to manifest according to the ancient vow and Scripture. The manifestations take on increasingly and eerily precise forms. In prior chapters we've shown how America's rise and spiritual fall paralleled the rise and apostasy of ancient Israel. We revealed how the ancient patterns and dynamics of Israel's rise and plunge have manifested themselves through Nine Harbingers.

We introduced and discussed five of these harbingers: the Breach, the Terrorist, the Bricks, the Tower, and the Gazit Stone. The Breach and the Terrorist provided the context for all subsequent harbingers. They represent God's response to a nation's continued rebellion by allowing His protective hedge to be breached through a sudden invasion by a terrorist adversary. This was a serious wake-up call to a people who had rejected every earlier call to repentance and return.

The Bricks, the Tower, and the Gazit Stone emerge from the opening sentence of Isaiah 9:10: "The bricks have fallen down, but we will rebuild with hewn stones." Together they represent Israel's response to the breach and the invasion, a response of rebellion and defiance rather than repentance, with a vow to rebuild bigger and better than before. Like the Breach and the Terrorist, we saw how these harbingers reappeared in America during and after the 9/11 attacks.

In this study we will explore the sign of the falling tree, the Sycamore, the act of *khalaf*, its replacement with the Erez Tree, the actual manifestations of the ancient vow of judgment by America's leaders, and the ominous meaning therein.

The Sixth Harbinger: The Sycamore

The sycamore of ancient Israel

> The bricks have fallen down, but we will rebuild with hewn [quarried] stones. The sycamores have been cut down, but we will plant cedars in their place.
>
> —Isaiah 9:10

The Sixth Harbinger is seen in the opening words of the second sentence of Isaiah 9:10. As in the case of the bricks falling, Israel is acknowledging that an invasion has happened and damage has occurred.

The Assyrians not only attacked and destroyed buildings but also destroyed the trees of the land, particularly the sycamores. The destruction of the sycamores is mentioned even in the account of Egypt's plagues. It's a sign of national judgment, a warning of national uprooting. The fallen bricks are a sign of destruction; the fallen sycamore is a sign of uprooting and death.

The American sycamore

AP Images / Stuart Ramson

The Hebrew word *shakam*, or fig-mulberry tree, is that from which the word *sycamore* comes. In Greek, *fig* is *sukos* and *mulberry* is *moros*, thus *sukomoros* or *sycamore*. The Hebrew version of the sycamore naturally grows in the Middle East but not in cooler climates like that of the American Northeast. But just as the Hebrew sycamore was endemic to Israel, so there is a western sycamore endemic to America. On 9/11 it was this tree that just happened to be growing at the corner of Ground Zero. The striking down of Israel's sycamore trees was a sign of national judgment. In a strange series of events, in the last moments of 9/11 a shock wave and a steel beam went forth from the falling north tower and struck down the tree. The tree became a symbol known as the "Sycamore of Ground Zero." The sycamore had fallen—the Sixth Harbinger.

The Seventh Harbinger:
The Erez Tree

The erez tree of ancient Israel

> The sycamores have been cut down, but we will plant cedars in
> their place.
> —ISAIAH 9:10, AUTHOR'S TRANSLATION

As in the case of the fallen bricks, Israel's noting the cutting down
of the sycamore is followed not by a turning to God, but by a defiant,
unrepentant vow to replace it with something larger or stronger. As the
bricks were replaced by quarried stone, so was the sycamore replaced by
a bigger and stronger cedar.

The Hebrew word in Isaiah 9:10 that's translated *cedar* is *erez*. It is
actually a conifer or coniferous tree. In a number of ancient texts it
refers to a particular kind of cone-bearing evergreen. The erez tree
would fall under the botanical classification of *pinacea*, which refers to
the spruce, the cedar, the pine, and the fir.

Thus the most accurate translation would be, "But we will plant
pinacea trees in their place."

The erez tree is the Seventh Harbinger.

The American erez tree

Margie Bibb

Has this sign of the erez tree been manifested in America? When the lone sycamore tree of Ground Zero fell, it was removed, including its root system, and put elsewhere on display. In November 2003, two years later, a ceremonial act took place at the corner of Ground Zero. A tree was lowered by crane into a specific spot of earth—the ground in which the Sycamore of Ground Zero had stood.

It was not another sycamore tree.

It was an evergreen conifer tree, literally a pinacea tree; it was a biblical "erez" tree, as referred to in the ancient vow of defiance.

And as with the case of the quarried stone or Gazit Stone replacing the bricks at Ground Zero, the erez tree replacing the sycamore was a public event, symbolizing national defiance instead of humility in response to an attack. The highly publicized new tree was even given a name: "The Ground Zero Tree of Hope."

The Eighth Harbinger: The Utterance

The utterance in Samaria

> The Lord sent a word against Jacob,
> And it has fallen on Israel.
> All the people will know—
> Ephraim and the inhabitant of Samaria—
> Who say in pride and arrogance of heart:
> The bricks have fallen down…
>
> —ISAIAH 9:8–10

We've seen how one scripture, Isaiah 9:10, explicitly contains the harbingers that tell ancient Israel's story, revealing patterns of defiance to God's will that are repeated in modern America. Containing the two previous verses of the chapter, the above passage, with its mention of Ephraim, confirms that the nation being mentioned is the northern kingdom of Israel. Its mention of Samaria, the kingdom's capital city, suggested that Israel's defiant vow was made there.

This points us to the Eighth Harbinger, the utterance of the vow—the whole of Isaiah 9:10—in the rebellious nation's capital city.

Simply stated, following a calamity caused by God lifting His hedge of protection on a backslidden nation, a nation's leaders respond with public defiance. They boast of their country's resolve and power. They speak of its fallen bricks and quarried stones, its uprooting trees and their replanting. They speak of a nation defiant and determined to emerge stronger than ever. The words become a vow. The vow gives voice to a national spirit and seals the nation's course. It all takes place in its capital city.

The American utterance

Has this harbinger, the Utterance, like the previous harbingers, been manifested in America? Yes.

It happened the late summer of 2004 during a presidential election campaign. By that time, the Erez Tree had replaced the sycamore and the Gazit Stone the fallen bricks. In other words, every object mentioned in Isaiah 9:10's ancient prophecy had manifested at Ground Zero.

The date was September 11, 2004. The event was the third anniversary of the 9/11 breach. The speaker was the senator and vice president candidate John Edwards. The place was America's capital city of Washington.

Speaking at a gathering of a congressional caucus, Edwards uttered these words:

Good morning. Today, on this day of remembrance and mourning,
we have the Lord's Word to get us through:

The bricks have fallen
But we will build with dressed stones
The sycamores have been cut down
But we will put cedars in their place.[1]

By quoting Isaiah 9:10, a major American candidate for high office
had precisely uttered Israel's ancient vow. He had meant it to be a positive inspiration to the audience. He or presumably his speechwriter
didn't read the context. No one realized that in quoting the text, he was
unwittingly highlighting America's defiance in response to calamity,
following the exact pattern set by Israel's original defiance revealed in
the text. In other words, the utterance joined the Assyrian invasion to
9/11 and America's post-9/11 defiance to Israel's defiance in the face of
God's judgment.

Even more amazing, the entire speech delivered that day was built
around that same ancient vow. Edwards took the objects of Isaiah 9:10,
the sycamore, the cedar or erez tree, and the hewn stone, and used
them as figures or symbols of 9/11, America's response to 9/11, and what
he believed to be national resurgence.

He said the following:

> Let me show you how we are building and putting cedars in those
> three hallowed places.[2]

He added this:

> And in a place where smoke once rose, you and I, we will see that
> cedar rising.[3]

And this:

> You will see that while those bricks fell and the sycamores cut
> down, our people are making those cedars rise.[4]

And then he came to his dramatic conclusion:

> The cedars will rise, the stones will go up, and this season of hope will endure.[5]

Intending to deliver an inspiring address, he was unwittingly pronouncing judgment on America. Like so many other American leaders, he was unknowingly performing his part of the mystery.

The Ninth Harbinger: The Prophecy

The prophetic vow of ancient Israel

Unlike any of the previous harbingers, the Eighth Harbinger isn't about a piece of the mystery of Isaiah 9:10 but the whole of it.

The same is true for the Ninth and final Harbinger.

There is, however, a difference between these harbingers. The Eighth Harbinger is about Isaiah 9:10 in present tense. It's about a nation uttering a vow in defiance of God. In the case of Edwards, it confirms what America is actually carrying out. But the Ninth Harbinger is Isaiah 9:10 purely spoken in the future tense. It's about a prophet, Isaiah, speaking God's word to the full nation, spotlighting its arrogant pride and rebellion and warning it through a sign foretelling its future.

The Ninth Harbinger is as follows: In the wake of calamity, the nation responds through a vow. The vow sets it on a rebellious course ending in judgment. The words of the vow become part of a prophetic revelation given to the whole nation, an indictment of it, a foretelling of its future, a warning of its judgment.

In other words, the Ninth and last Harbinger is especially prophetic in foretelling what is yet to happen.

When did ancient Israel utter the words of Isaiah 9:10, which became prophecy? It undoubtedly did so soon after the calamity, the Assyrian invasion.

The Capitol Hill prophetic vow

Has this final harbinger, the Prophecy, like all of the ones preceding it, reappeared in America? Yes.

On the morning of September 12, 2001, a day after America's calamity, the al Qaeda breach, the US Senate and House of Representatives, the

representative bodies of the entire American nation, issued a joint resolution in response to 9/11.

After the resolution was read, condemning the attacks, expressing
condolences, and calling for unity, a war against the terrorists, and punishment of the guilty parties, the Senate majority leader, Tom Daschle,
the highest representative of the nation's highest legislative body, rose
to speak.

At the end of the speech, Daschle uttered the following:

> I know that there is only the smallest measure of inspiration that
> can be taken from this devastation, but there is a passage in the
> Bible from Isaiah that I think speaks to all of us at times like
> this....
>
> The bricks have fallen down,
> But we will rebuild with dressed stone;
> The fig trees have been felled,
> But we will replace them with cedars.[6]

Thus the words of Israel's ancient vow were officially joined to
America and 9/11. Just as Isaiah's recording of the vow transformed
into a matter of Israel's national record and a prophetic word for all the
people, so now the same words were officially recorded in the Annals of
Congress as a matter of America's national record.

As with Senator Edwards three years later, Daschle said these words
without realizing what he was saying. And yet there was a prophetic
dimension to the occurrence. He spoke of a fallen tree that he knew
nothing about, but which was discovered in the days after 9/11. He
spoke of the act of replacing the one tree with the other. That would
happen two years later. He spoke of the Gazit Stone that would go up
in the rebuilding of Ground Zero, and it would happen three years later.

How can a man who is not a prophet speak prophetically? The Bible
gives the answer. Men who are not prophets and who may even not
know God or, in some cases, be against Him may speak prophetically and say things on two levels without even realizing what they're
saying. So the Gospels record that this very thing happened in the case

of Caiaphas when he plotted the murder of Yeshua, Jesus. Yet the very words of the plot had another meaning: that it was necessary for one man to die as a sacrifice so that the people would not perish.

Daschle's closing vow of "That is what we will do"[7] was referring to none other than the ancient vow of judgment. Thus he was saying, unwittingly, that America would follow in the ominous footsteps of ancient Israel. America as a nation would carry out the vow of Isaiah 9:10. His words would indeed be prophetic. As this is exactly what America would do.

WEEK 5 EXPLORE *and* APPLY

Read chapters 10–13 of *The Harbinger.*

Watch or listen to the accompanying resource, *The Harbinger I* DVD or CD from *The Harbinger: The Full Revelation* eight-disc album.

Read Isaiah 1:1–18; Isaiah 9:10; 2 Kings 17:7–14.

▧ *Explore* ▧

In Isaiah 1:1–18 the Lord is trying to turn His people back to Himself. How do you think He is doing it? What is His heart in the matter? How do you think people at the time could misinterpret His actions with regard to the nation?

Look at 2 Kings 17:7–14. Use this as a template through which to view what is happening now in Isaiah 9:10 regarding the harbingers the Breach, the Sycamore, the Erez Tree, the Utterance, and the Prophecy. How do 2 Kings 17 and Isaiah 9:10 go together? (Keep in mind it's talking about the same nation and ultimately the same general time period.)

The Sycamore

In what ways could the sycamores of Israel have been struck down by the Assyrian armies?

The fall of Egypt in the Book of Exodus is the first fully displayed judgment of a nation recorded in Scripture. Can you find in Scripture where this judgment involved the destruction of the sycamore?

In Isaiah 9:10 the fallen sycamore is a sign of national judgment. Where else can you find in Scripture the image of a tree cut down, fallen as a sign of national judgment? (There are more than one.)

Was the sycamore a highly valued tree?

In how many ways is the striking down of a tree different from the destruction of a building?

How is the warning contained in this different from the warning of a destroyed building?

Why would it appear unlikely for the sign of the sycamore to be manifested in, of all places, New York City?

On September 11, 2001, in the wake of the attack, an object was struck down by the falling tower. The object was a tree, the sycamore, the American or western variety of the tree. How many things had to be in exact place for this to happen?

What could such a sign mean for America?

The Erez Tree

The Israelites vow to plant trees in the same place where once stood the sycamores. Why is the planting in the same exact spot significant? And what is it significant of?

The Israelites choose the biblical erez tree to replace the sycamore. The erez tree commonly referred to the cedar, but the word also is used in the Bible to speak of trees in the desert. But the cedar doesn't grow in the desert. What does that tell us about the word?

Erez refers to a family of trees including the cedar, the spruce, and the fir. These are all evergreens. What significance could that hold for the Israelites choosing this to replace the sycamores?

The word *erez* comes from *araz*, which means firm or strong. How is this significant in the context of Isaiah 9:10?

The erez tree grew taller than the sycamore, was more majestic, more valuable, and more highly prized. So by replacing the fallen sycamore with the erez tree, what were the Hebrews saying to God?

Compare the two phrases of the vow: "The bricks have fallen, but we will rebuild with hewn stone," and "The sycamores have been cut down, but we will plant cedars in their place." How many parallels can you find between the two parts of the vow?

The Utterance

The speaking of the vow itself was a sign of defiance. Many may have spoken such words—but what group of people in particular would have had to have uttered such a vow on behalf of the entire nation and to set the nation's course?

Where did the leaders of Israel's northern kingdom reside? What was the capital city?

What was wrong with such a vow?

What was it in the historical context, in Israel's situation at the time, that made the vow an ominous mistake?

How do we know that the utterance was spoken in a wrongful spirit, in arrogance?

How important does God feel this vow was, and what were the consequences of its being made?

On September 11, 2004, an American senator gave a speech in the capital city, Washington DC, and out of his mouth proceeded the ancient vow of defiance and judgment, word for word. How could he have done this? What was he thinking when he proclaimed Isaiah 9:10 to begin his speech?

What was he thinking he was saying? What was he actually saying?

The speech was given in Washington DC, the capital, and on the anniversary of 9/11. Why are both factors significant?

The Prophecy

What is it about the vow that would tell us that it had to have been first said soon after the attack on Israel?

How did the vow become part of the national record?

Once the words are recorded in the Book of Isaiah, how do they take on a double meaning:

- One, the meaning that the leaders who proclaimed it intended it to have

- Two, the meaning they had prophetically, and ironically, as words of self-proclaimed judgment

Beyond the actual stones and trees of the vow, what was the nation vowing to do—and in how many ways do you think Israel sought to fulfill the vow?

Would their efforts be successful? What is it in the scriptural context that tells us that they would fail?

On the day after 9/11, the American Congress gathered on Capitol Hill to issue its response to the attack. Why might this response be especially significant or even prophetic?

The man appointed to give this response and speak for the nation was the Senate majority leader. What is it about that position that is especially representative to allow him to speak on behalf of the entire nation?

The Senate majority leader closed his speech by reciting the ancient vow in Isaiah. What was he intending to do by quoting from Isaiah?

What was significant about the fact that when he spoke that vow, he was referring to an attack on the nation?

At the end of his speech the Senate majority leader said, "That is what we will do." He was referring to the words of Isaiah 9:10. He was saying that America would do as ancient Israel had done. Why was that an ominous thing to say?

In what ways did America follow the footsteps of ancient Israel after 9/11?

◼ *Spiritual Truths* ◼

How many ways or means can you think of in which God has spoken to man in the Bible?

How many different ways can you cite in which God warned a nation of judgment?

How many signs can you identify that God gave in the Bible to warn or speak to a nation of judgment?

■ *Mission to Apply This Week* ■

The most important message that God can send to an unbeliever is the message of the gospel, salvation.

Who needs to hear this message in your life? In the space provided, write down a mission for this week concerning those in your life who need to hear the gospel—committing yourself to sharing with them, those you already know and those you may not know but will meet this week.

Take time now to commit this to God and pray for His help and anointing.

Seal this commitment in prayer (individually, in small groups, as a class, or congregationally).

Prepare for next week (groups only): This week read, go over, and explore the next chapter, "The Isaiah 9:10 Effect."

▨ *Write Down* ▨

1. Your thoughts, notes, and insights

2. What you believe the Lord is calling you to do

3. Your mission for the days ahead

Chapter 6

The ISAIAH 9:10 EFFECT

The Second Shaking

IN OUR SERIES of studies we have gone through all Nine Harbingers—the Breach, the Terrorist, the Bricks, the Tower, the Gazit Stone, the Sycamore, the Erez Tree, the Utterance, and the Prophecy. We have seen how, twenty-seven centuries after first appearing to Israel's northern kingdom in its last days as a nation in the face of judgment, they have now reappeared in America, a nation conceived after the pattern of ancient Israel and now following in the same fateful footsteps.

The harbingers appeared in ancient Israel and reappeared in America only after God's calls to repentance had fallen on deaf ears. The Breach and the Terrorist resulted from God removing His hedge of protection on Israel and later America, allowing a serious attack from an outside enemy, leaving visible but limited damage in its wake. The seven succeeding harbingers involve the response to the attack and the divine warning it communicated. It was a response of defiance, superficially to the attackers but on a deeper level to God.

But what happens when the harbingers aren't heeded? There then comes a second stage.

In the case of ancient Israel, the Assyrian attack on the land was not the end but the beginning of a progression of national warnings, shakings, and judgments. The commentaries almost universally identify the dynamic: As a nation rejects the warnings of initial shakings, more will come. In fact, it will bring more about. In the next few studies we will explore the underlying biblical dynamics and the ancient mysteries concerning this phenomenon, something that has radically altered the American and global economy: the second shaking.

Isaiah 9:11

Isaiah 9:10 records ancient Israel's vow of defiance in response to the Assyrian attack through which God was seeking to warn the nation and spur it to repentance. But in the very next verse following the vow is the starting point of something else:

> Therefore, the LORD shall set up
> The adversaries of Rezin against him,
> And spur his enemies on.

In other words, the vow leads to a progressive manifestation of national calamity and judgment. The historical context for Isaiah 9:10–11 may be summed up as follows: Despite being blessed by God with decades of unparalleled peace and prosperity, the northern kingdom had refused to turn from its worship of the foreign gods of its neighbors and its embrace of their sinful practices. By the middle 700s BC, Assyria's meteoric rise to the north was itself a warning, a sign of the unmistakable end of an era. Yet even after the Assyrians breached Israel's defenses, Israel responded not with repentance but with vows to rebuild bigger and better than ever, and it began converting those vows into action. As the rebuilding accelerated, so did the nation's trust in its own strength.

Meanwhile, both before and after the Assyrian breach, Israel turned to foreign powers, from King Pekah's alliance with Syria's king, Rezin, to King Hoshea's entreaties to So, the king of Egypt. Both moves were meant to strengthen Israel's hand against Assyria. But Pekah's alliance with Rezin led to their invasion of Judah, which called on Assyria for help, provoking Assyria's invasion of the northern kingdom in 732 BC. And Hoshea's attempted conspiracy against Assyria led to Assyria's taking Hoshea captive and to the final destruction of the northern kingdom a decade later.

The Isaiah 9:10 Effect

At play is a paradoxical or ironic dynamic that may be called the Isaiah 9/10 Effect: the attempt of a nation to defy the course of its judgment, apart from repentance, will instead set in motion a chain of events to bring about the very calamity it sought to avert.

Israel's very attempts to defend against the threat posed by Assyria, undertaken without any repentance, without any return to God or altering of its national course, would ultimately lead to national destruction. All that it had done in the years after the initial Assyrian invasion (732 BC) to build itself up in power and defense would come crashing down in 722 BC like a house of cards. The nation's attempt to defy God's chastening judgments would end up triggering the very calamity the nation had sought to avert.

What was true of ancient Israel is true of America. As with Israel, in the years after 9/11 America took action on its vow to rebuild and become stronger and securer than ever. Besides its efforts at Ground Zero and across lower Manhattan, it established a new Department of

Homeland Security and launched a global war on terror as well as wars in Iraq and Afghanistan.

But as was the case with Israel, America's attempts to rebuild floundered without dealing with its spiritual and moral descent. As Isaiah 9:10 became America's post-9/11 domestic and foreign policy, the Isaiah 9/10 Effect was set into motion.

The attempts to strengthen America's national security and defenses required tremendous expenditures. The War on Terror and military campaigns in Afghanistan and Iraq would add hundreds of billions of dollars to the budget. The war in Iraq would impel a surge in oil prices. All of this spending led to the skyrocketing national debt.

Six Days After: We Will Rebuild

In addition, six days after the 9/11 attack in an attempt to stave off a potential post-9/11 economic debacle, the Federal Reserve began the first of a series of historic interest-rate reductions that would force the rate below that of inflation. This was the equivalent of creating free money.

These moves led to a chain of economic events that ironically led to the calamity they were attempting to avoid. Rock-bottom interest rates meant easy loans, borrowing, and mortgages. Easier mortgages created an unprecedented housing and building boom. As the value of their houses inflated, homeowners borrowed and spent against them, creating credit bubbles across the economy. Massive inflows from Asia compounded the problem. The stock market surged. Meanwhile, central banks across the globe slashed their interest rates repeatedly, with similar results to America's.

Since the economic boom was linked to Isaiah 9:10 and America's attempt to beat back the effects of 9/11, the Isaiah 9:10 Effect kicked in, and the nation's "resurgence" turned out to be a hollow illusion. It all collapsed.

The credit explosion led to a debt explosion. Standard cautions and restraints involved in borrowing and lending were thrown away.

Personal, government, and corporate debt skyrocketed. Investment and banking firms engaged in increasingly risky practices.

The House of Cards Collapses

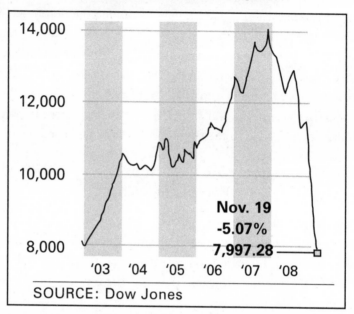

SOURCE: Dow Jones

In September 2008, seven years after the 9/11 attacks, America's financial system began to implode, resulting in the greatest economic disaster since the Great Depression. As the house of cards began collapsing in America, it affected the world.

The connection between 9/11 and the economic implosion was clear:

> We can trace the roots of the crisis back to the 9/11 terror attacks…[Greenspan] kept on cutting the interest rates after September 11…[1]

> The financial house of cards was slowly built following the 9/11 attacks…[2]

In other words, behind the collapse of the American economy, the crash of Wall Street, and the Great Recession lies an ancient principle of national judgment, the Isaiah 9:10 Effect. And its meaning for the future is that if America does not return to God, does not turn her course toward repentance, her problem will never be solved by any other means—economic, political, military, or any other means. The shaking of the nation will continue.

WEEK 6 EXPLORE *and* APPLY

Read chapters 14 and 15 of *The Harbinger.*

Watch or listen to the accompanying resource *The Isaiah 9:10 Effect* DVD or CD from *The Harbinger: The Full Revelation* eight-disc album.

Read Isaiah 9:11–18.

▦ *Explore* ▦

What scriptural examples of people who sought to solve spiritual problems by using nonspiritual solutions can you think of?

What exactly was the northern kingdom of Israel embarking on as proclaimed in the vow? Was it just about stones and trees?

How do you think they sought to strengthen themselves, particularly in these realms:

- Rebuilding the nation
- Walls of defense
- Strategic alliances
- Their military
- Trusting in other gods

Do you think that for a time Israel may have had the appearance of national resurgence?

How did the "spirit of defiance," the same spirit that led them to make the vow, ultimately lead to their destruction?

What was God's answer in Isaiah 9:11 to ancient Israel's vow of defiance in Isaiah 9:10?

What is the Isaiah 9:10 Effect?

Why is it that Israel could not solve its problems militarily, economically, or strategically?

How is it like a man who tries to kill a weed by cutting of its stem?

After 9/11 American leaders not only vowed the same vow as ancient Israel but also set forth national policy in the same direction as that of ancient Israel. See if you can identify modern equivalents to what ancient Israel did in what America did after 9/11:

- Rebuilding the nation
- Walls of defense
- Strategic alliances
- Their military
- Trusting in other gods (or powers or things)

What were the unintended consequences of this general campaign to undo the effects of 9/11 without returning to God?

How did the economic collapse of America begin with 9/11 and the nation's "Isaiah 9:10 reaction" to it?

What does the Isaiah 9:10 Effect and the example of ancient Israel signify for America if the nation does not return to God?

■ *Spiritual Truths* ■

Can we apply the Isaiah 9:10 Effect to the lives of individuals?

What happens when a person tries to solve a spiritual problem or problems that have to do with their relationship or lack of relationship with God by other means?

■ *Mission to Apply This Week* ■

Is there a problem or issue in your life that you've been dealing with for years? In light of what we've learned about fixing problems without repenting, does it change the way you might need to solve or resolve the problem?

What step can you take this week to solve it once and for all with God? Write it down in the space provided, and make this your mission.

Take time now to commit this to God and pray for His help and anointing.

Seal this commitment in prayer (individually, in small groups, as a class, or congregationally).

Prepare for next week (groups only): This week read, go over, and explore the next chapter, "The Uprooted."

■ *Write Down* ■

1. Your thoughts, notes, and insights

2. What you believe the Lord is calling you to do

3. Your mission for the days ahead

Chapter 7

The UPROOTED

The Foundations Laid Bare

IN THE DAYS of judgment, foundations are exposed. What are the foundations on which a nation rests? How are they laid bare? What are the foundations on which we rest our lives? What is the foundation of America's rise as the world's financial superpower? This study explores the meaning of foundations and their exposing and the mystery that marks the day America began its rise to the world's financial colossus.

What is a foundation? It is that upon which something else stands, rests, or is built. When the context concerns a nation, the foundation can either be that on which the nation was established or that on which the nation places its ultimate trust. It can range from the one true God to counterfeit gods, ranging from literal idols to military prowess or economic strength.

> So I will break down the wall you have plastered with untempered mortar, and bring it down to the ground, so that its foundation will be uncovered; it will fall, and you shall be consumed in the midst of it. Then you shall know that I am the LORD.
> —EZEKIEL 13:14

In Ezekiel 13:14 God is saying that when the nation is judged, its foundation will be exposed for all to see.

The Bible gives various examples of God's judgment of a nation that worships false gods. In the judgment of Egypt, when Pharaoh repeatedly refused to let the children of Israel go, as seen in chapters 7 through 12 of the Book of Exodus, God replied with a succession of ten plagues, each corresponding to a counterfeit Egyptian god. Taken together, the plagues exposed Egypt's faulty foundation, revealing the impotence of its false deities. Likewise, when God judged Babylon, the gods, or that in which the Babylonians had put their trust, would be judged.

In Ezekiel 13:14 God warns Israel that He will expose her false foundations—the foundations of reliance and trust in power, alliances, false gods, false prophets, and idols. He would tear the nation down to her foundations.

The Breaking and the Uprooting

At the same time, unlike other nations, beneath Israel's false foundations was its true and original one. God was its builder and planter. Thus, when God judged Israel, He tore down what He had built and uprooted that which He had planted. In so doing, He exposed Israel's new but false foundation.

> Behold, what I have built I will *break down*, and what I have planted, I will *pluck up* [uproot].
> —JEREMIAH 45:4, EMPHASIS ADDED

The pattern of biblical judgment first involves a breaking down and then an uprooting. So note the resemblance to Isaiah 9:10:

> The bricks have fallen...the sycamores have been cut down.
> —ISAIAH 9:10

On 9/11 the collapse of the towers was followed by the uprooting of the sycamore tree. Recall these words of Ezekiel 13:14 above:

> I will break down the wall...and bring it down to the ground...

The Rising Power

The World Trade Center symbolized America's financial power, one that was centuries in the making and long connected with Manhattan Island. At the dawn of the seventeenth century the island was a trading post for the Dutch, who built a wall against perceived threats. The wall became Manhattan's center of trade and commerce. Eventually the British took the island and tore down the wall. But a nearby road continued to bear the name of "Wall Street," which became the embodiment of a new nation's financial prowess and, eventually, the financial capital of the world.

How did this transformation happen? In March 1792 Manhattan's leading merchants convened secretly at a hotel to discuss bringing order to the trading of stocks and bonds. On May 17 of that year they met again at 68 Wall Street to sign a document.

Buttonwood

The document was named the *Buttonwood Agreement.* The organization it birthed was called the *Buttonwood Association,* eventually renamed the *New York Stock Exchange.* The word *buttonwood* referred to a tree on Wall Street under which the merchants met.

Another word for buttonwood is *sycamore.*

Wall Street and American financial power began under a syca-more tree—the Sixth Harbinger, birthing a Buttonwood or Sycamore Agreement and a Buttonwood or Sycamore Association, later to be known as the New York Stock Exchange. Thus the original symbol of Wall Street and America's rise to financial superpower status is the sycamore.

While the World Trade Center symbolized what America's financial strength had become, the sycamore was the symbol of its original foundation. And growing in the shadow of the World Trade Center was the Sycamore of Ground Zero.

The Tree as a Biblical Sign

In the Bible God often uses the image of a tree to stand as a symbol of a nation. Babylon is spoken of as a tree, as is Assyria, as is Israel. A tree is like a nation in that it is, in effect, planted, in that it grows, in that it branches out, produces fruit, and has a lifespan. At the same time the destroying or uprooting of a tree speaks of the judgment of a nation. So the Lord would speak of national judgment in the form of the destruction of a tree:

> The Lord called your name, Green Olive Tree, Lovely, and of Good Fruit. With the noise of a great tumult He has kindled a fire

on it, and its branches are broken. For the LORD of Hosts, who planted you, has pronounced doom against you.

—JEREMIAH 11:16–17

The Sycamore Fallen

On 9/11 the symbol of America's rise as a global economic superpower, the sycamore, reappeared in a different form, now fallen. A statue of the uprooted sycamore was made in bronze and placed, not at Ground Zero, but at the end of Wall Street.

So in the place where America's rise to financial superpower began, the place symbolized and named after a living sycamore tree, now appeared the image memorialized in bronze of a sycamore uprooted, the Sixth Harbinger, the Sycamore of Ground Zero.

It was the fall of the World Trade Center—the symbol of what American financial and economic power had become—that struck down the sycamore. In like manner, the 9/11 attack caused the collapse of Wall Street and America's economy, both immediately after the calamity and then through unleashing a myriad of reactions that would lead to the collapse of Wall Street and the American economy seven years later.

In other words, the uprooting of the sycamore wasn't just a warning of judgment, but it was also a foreshadowing of the uprooting of America's unparalleled financial and economic prosperity.

If a living sycamore signifies the rise of America as the world's pre-eminent financial power, an uprooted sycamore signifies its fall. God had allowed America's power to be planted, take root and grow on Wall Street, and branch out to the world, rising to unprecedented heights of global power and prosperity. But as America turned from His will and ways, a sign was manifested.

If America refused to turn back, the blessings symbolized by the sycamore would be removed, that which had been built up would be broken down, and that which had been planted would be uprooted.

WEEK 7 EXPLORE *and* APPLY

Read chapter 16 of *The Harbinger.*

Watch or listen to the accompanying resource *The Uprooted* DVD or CD from *The Harbinger: The Full Revelation* eight-disc album.

Read Ezekiel 13:14; Jeremiah 45:4; Jeremiah 11:16–17.

▪ *Explore* ▪

Why does judgment involve exposing foundations?

How did the judgment of Egypt expose its foundations?

In a physical picture, when would the foundation of a house or building become totally exposed?

How many places in the Bible can you think of where a tree is used by God as a symbol?

How is a tree a good symbol of the nation of Israel? How can it be a symbol of other nations?

What other times can you recall the Bible using the image or symbol of a tree to speak of or foreshadow judgment?

What would the symbol of the uprooting of a tree mean for both Israel (the northern kingdom) and Judah (the southern kingdom)? How would the meaning of uprooting come true for them?

How is one of the harbingers not only a sign of judgment but also a specific sign linked to America's foundation?

Why might it be appropriate to call Wall Street, "Sycamore"?

The force of 9/11 uprooted a sycamore tree. In what way is this image prophetic of what happened seven years later to the American economy?

What is a bit strange or different about the statue of the Sycamore of Ground Zero?

Where is the foundation of America's financial power located?

What is striking about the fact that the statue of an uprooted sycamore tree was placed at the end of Wall Street?

What might the symbol of uprooting suggest?

■ *Spiritual Truths* ■

How can an uprooted America be replanted in its original biblical soil?

The Bible speaks of individuals also as trees. How is an individual like a tree?

■ *Mission to Apply This Week* ■

God called you to be like a tree, with strong and deep roots in Him and bearing eternal fruit. What fruit specifically do you believe God has called your life to bear?

Are you bearing it?

How can you become more strongly and deeply rooted in God and His life so that you might bear the fruit He has called your life to bear?

What steps can you take this week toward that purpose? Write it down as a mission in the space provided.

Take time now to commit this to God and pray for His help and anointing.

Seal this commitment in prayer (individually, in small groups, as a class, or congregationally).

Prepare for next week (groups only): This week read, go over, and explore the next chapter, "The Mystery of the Shemitah."

▧ *Write Down* ▧

1. Your thoughts, notes, and insights

2. What you believe the Lord is calling you to do

3. Your mission for the days ahead

Chapter 8

The MYSTERY *of the* SHEMITAH

The Seventh Year

God gave Israel a unique command: every seven years its people were to rest. It was to be a Sabbath year—the Shemitah. Israel's observance or defiance of this ordinance would be a sign of its relationship to God and would determine its destiny. What happens when a nation that once knew God and His rest now drives Him out of its life? What happens when a believer does the same? This study will explore the mystery of the Shemitah as a sign of judgment against a nation that has driven God out of its life and its striking significance for America.

> When you come into the land which I give you, then the land shall keep a sabbath unto the LORD. Six years you shall sow your field, and six years you shall prune your vineyard, and gather its fruit; but in the seventh year there shall be a sabbath of solemn rest for the land, a sabbath to the LORD.
>
> —LEVITICUS 25:2–4

Just as God commanded ancient Israel to keep the seventh day of the week as a day of rest, so did God command His people at Sinai to give the land they were to enter a rest. It was called the *Shemitah*, meaning "the release," "the remission," or "the letting rest." Every seventh year the fruits of the harvest were abandoned. (See Leviticus 25:5.)

> Six years you shall sow your land and gather its produce, but the seventh year you shall let it rest and lie fallow, that the poor of your people may eat.
>
> —EXODUS 23:10–11

Every seventh year God required the opening up of land to those in need. The poor would share equally with the rich. The land's yield would become the possession of all.

Elul 29

The Shemitah touched not just land but also people:

> At the end of every seven years you shall grant a release of debts. And this is the form of the release: Every creditor who has lent anything to his neighbor shall release it; he shall not require it of his neighbor or his brother, because it is called the LORD's release [Shemitah].
>
> —DEUTERONOMY 15:1–2

So at the end of every seventh year, which was the twenty-ninth day of the biblical month of Elul, all debts were canceled; the nation's financial accounts were nullified.

The effects and repercussions of the Shemitah extend into the financial realm, the economic realm, and the realms of labor, employment, production, consumption, and trade. It would cause much of these things to cease or greatly diminish, and in the case of Elul 29, the wiping away of all credit and debt would nullify much of the nation's financial realm.

Thus, the Shemitah in many ways had the outward appearance of an economic collapse. In fact, the financial and economic ramifications were so radical that the rabbis sought ways to get around it with such practices as selling land to non-Jewish people during the period affected or replacing symbolic actions and transactions instead of financial ones. The Shemitah remains one of the most unique ordinances in the Bible in its massive effect and repercussions on a nation's financial and economic realm.

The Blessing Turns Into a Sign of Judgment

As a year of release and freedom, rest from one's labors, and drawing near to the Lord, God meant the Shemitah year as a blessing. But ancient Israel rebelled and abandoned both the Sabbath and the Shemitah. The breaking of the Shemitah constituted a sign of the nation's ruling God out of her life, driving Him out of her fields, labor, government, culture, homes, and life. Rather than serving the God of rest, the nation now served foreign idols and knew no rest, only the relentless pursuit of increase and gain.

Created to be a blessing, the Shemitah, in its breaking, would become a judgment. It would still come, but now in the form of national calamity. In the days of Jeremiah, foreign armies would seize the land, ravage the cities and fields, take the people captive into exile, and the land would rest. Commerce would stop. Every debt would be obliterated.

Seventy Years of Shemitahs

In pursuit of prosperity the people drove God and the Shemitah out of the land. But now it was the Shemitah that drove them out of the land, nullifying all of their gains.

This was foretold at Sinai, when the ordinance of the Shemitah was given:

> Your land shall be desolate and your cities waste. Then the land shall enjoy its sabbaths as long as it lies desolate and you are in your enemies' land.... As long as it lies desolate it shall rest—for the time it did not rest on your sabbaths when you dwelt in it.
> —LEVITICUS 26:33–35

Centuries after Sinai, when Babylon's armies captured the land and took the people into captivity, this would be fulfilled. The exile lasted seventy years, representing the number of Sabbath years not kept:

> And those who escaped from the sword [King Nebuchadnezzar] carried away to Babylon...to fulfill the word of the LORD by the mouth of Jeremiah, until the land had enjoyed her Sabbaths. As long as she lay desolate she kept Sabbath, to fulfill seventy years.
> —2 CHRONICLES 36:20–21

The American Shemitah

The law of the Shemitah was given to Israel. America was never under obligation to observe a Sabbath year. But the Shemitah remains a biblical *sign* of judgment on a nation that has driven God out of its life and replaced Him with idols and the ceaseless pursuit of gain. Thus, it is the Shemitah as a biblical sign of national judgment in the context of the warning of America that now concerns us.

Behind the crash of Wall Street and the collapse of the American economy lies the mystery of the Shemitah.

In 2008 the collapse of Lehman Brothers and America's economy took place over the course of a week, the anniversary week of 9/11. Fannie Mae and Freddie Mac collapsed on September 7 of that year. Two days later Lehman Brothers began its fall, and on September 11, 2008, the stock market took a precipitous plunge.

Exactly seven years separated the two events, the precise biblical period of time that concerns the Shemitah. The economic collapse, from housing to finance, concerned a forced wiping away of the nation's financial accounts—the outward form of the Shemitah. In the case of Fannie Mae and Freddie Mac, the government relieved them of debts exceeding $5 trillion. In the case of Lehman Brothers, its bankruptcy wiped away its debts and canceled its loans.

All of these events helped trigger a stock market crash, touching the whole world and wiping out all gains over the preceding seven years and then some. The 2008 global economic collapse was one colossal Shemitah, made up of countless smaller ones.

The Great Collapse

On September 29, 2008, after a proposed economic and financial bailout failed to pass Congress, stocks plunged by more than 700 points. As one market analyst said:

> It was this event more than anything else that shattered market confidence. Over the next two weeks, the Dow fell close to 2700 points, a decline of almost 25 percent...the damage had been done.[1]

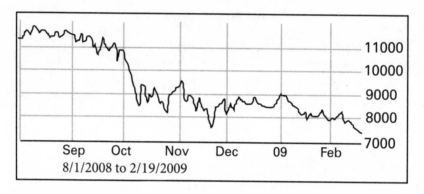

The greatest collapse of the 2008 economic implosion and the greatest stock market crash in American history happened on September 29, 2008. That day on the biblical calendar was the twenty-ninth day of Elul, the final, crowning day of the Hebrew Shemitah—and the exact day appointed by God for the wiping away of a nation's financial accounts.

The Shemitah revolves around the number seven. So the number seven arises over and over again concerning the economic collapse of 2008. The great collapse happened on the crowning day of the seventh year. It was triggered on Capitol Hill when Congress rejected a $700 billion bailout plan. Seven percent of the market was wiped out. And the number of points wiped away was 777.[2]

In order to trigger all of these "sevens," all of Wall Street, the American and world economies, every economic and financial transaction, had to be an exact position for it all to happen as it did, at the exact time and to that exact number. No human hand could have orchestrated it.

In the years preceding America's equivalent of the Shemitah year of 2008, the nation enjoyed a boom touching every area, from finance to the stock market to housing. But as America moved closer to that final year, danger signs began to surface, as loan failures and housing foreclosures rose.

Tishri 1: The Opening Day

But the first concrete sign of what was to come took place a year before the global economic collapse. In September 2007, Northern Rock, Britain's fifth largest mortgage lender, collapsed. It was the first British institution to suffer a bank run in more than a century. By the end of the crisis, Northern Rock would be nationalized—a remission of debt, a first Shemitah.

Northern Rock's fall happened on September 13, 2007, which on the biblical calendar is Tishri 1—the very day that opens up the Shemitah year. In other words, the first major sign of the Shemitah took place on the exact day on which the Shemitah begins. The fall of Northern Rock was linked to Lehman Brothers. It would be the fall of Lehman Brothers one year later that would trigger the collapse of the American economy.

From the day of Northern Rock's fall to the day of the greatest stock market crash in history we have the exact start and finish to the biblical year of Shemitah.

Within that year, from September 2007 to September 2008, the year's long climb of the stock market was reversed and the market began and then continued its fall. Many billions in stock market wealth were wiped out. Credit markets tightened, housing prices plunged, and foreclosures rose. As homeowners defaulted, the firms behind their mortgages absorbed cascading losses. This triggered more crises as lending institutions failed.

Each failure, each plunge, each bankruptcy constituted a wiping away of financial accounts, in outward form, a Shemitah, in this case a colossal Shemitah that overtook the world. And just as the biblical Shemitah touched the realms of labor, commerce, production, consumption, and trade—so did the economic implosion.

The Seven-Year Mystery

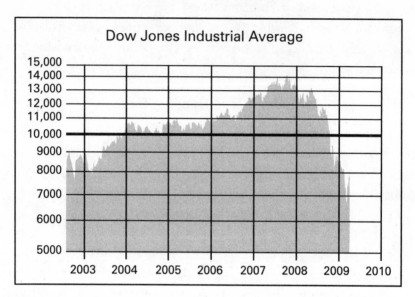

The Shemitah revolves around a seven-year cycle, and Elul 29 marks the end of that seven-year period. So what happens if we start from Elul 29, 2008, the date of the greatest collapse in Wall Street history, and go back seven Hebrew, biblical years?

It would bring us to Elul 29 of the year 2001. Did anything striking happen on that day? The answer is stunning. Elul 29 of 2001 was the day of the other greatest stock market crash in American history. Thus, on the biblical calendar, the two greatest stock market crashes in American history up to those days took place on the exact same Hebrew day, on the precise day appointed to touch a nation's financial realm and wipe out its financial accounts, and exactly seven years apart to the biblical day and hours—just as ordained in the Bible.

The day of the Shemitah in 2001 was September 17, 2001. Since this move, along with subsequent actions in the military and security realms, led to the economic calamity in 2008 seven years later, it is accurate to say that what began on the day of the Shemitah was the Isaiah 9:10 Effect:

The attempt of a nation to defy the course of its judgment, apart from repentance, will, instead, set into motion a chain of events to bring about the very calamity it sought to avert.

While the twenty-ninth of Elul comes around once a year, there is only one Elul 29 that can close the seven-year cycle and constitute the final day of the cycle's final year. Amazingly, the stock market crash of September 29, 2008, happened on precisely that one day in seven years that constitutes the biblical Shemitah. And as for the stock market collapse of 2001, it happened on the same one-in-seven-years biblical day.

In other words, America's two greatest stock market crashes not only happened on the same day on the biblical calendar, but they also happened on the one day of the biblical year ordained to wipe away credit. And they happened not just seven years apart to the day, but also on the exact once-in-seven-years occurrence of that one Hebrew day.

Since religious Jews continue to mark the Shemitah, this means that on the very day of the stock market crash, they were unwittingly bearing witness to its significance through their ritual acts of symbolically wiping away credits and debts, even as it was literally occurring on Wall Street.

The Sign of the Shemitah and America

The economic collapse of 2001 was caused by 9/11. That means that even the timing of 9/11 had to be woven into the mystery of the Shemitah. Moreover, for the crash of 2008 to have happened exactly seven biblical years later to the day, all of the key events, from the fall of Lehman Brothers to the vote on Capitol Hill to the Federal Reserve's actions, to the global crisis and every other event which affected the economic realm, had to be part of the same ancient mystery.

Finally, the Hebrew word *Shemitah* has still another meaning: *the fall* or *the letting fall*. So the Shemitah year may be called "the year of the letting fall." And everything that took place in the global economic collapse—from the housing market, to credit, to commerce, to economic indicators, etc.—constituted a *fall*. And it all began with the fall of Lehman Brothers, which was literally a *"letting fall,"* since the Federal Reserve literally had decided to *let it fall*. The entire global collapse began with America's government performing an act of Shemitah.

And yet, neither the government nor any other human agency could have possibly orchestrated the countless actions, reactions, and transactions that caused everything to happen precisely as it did at the exact times ordained in the ancient mystery. Thus, ultimately, it must be viewed as God's Shemitah—His *letting it fall*.

Given to ancient Israel as a blessing, the Shemitah became a curse through disobeying it. For America, it was a sign that as a nation it had forgotten its foundations, trusted in its own power and riches, and ruled God out of its life.

In the stunning facts and realities that lie beneath the two greatest collapses in American history, originating with 9/11, we find not only a sign of judgment but also a warning and foreshadow that if America does not return to God, her prosperity, her blessings, her financial and economic global preeminence—the American age as we know it—will also be *allowed to fall*.

WEEK 8 EXPLORE *and* APPLY

Read chapter 17 of *The Harbinger*.

Watch or listen to the accompanying resource *The Mystery of the Shemitah I and II*, two DVDs/CDs from *The Harbinger: The Full Revelation* eight-disc album.

Read Leviticus 25:2–5; 26:33–35; Exodus 23:10–11; Deuteronomy 15:1–2; 2 Chronicles 36:20–21.

■ *Explore* ■

What was the purpose of the Shemitah or Sabbath year?

What were the key commands or observances of the Shemitah?

What happened on the twenty-ninth day of the biblical month of Elul?

What is it in Deuteronomy 15:1–2 that reveals these verses are speaking about Elul 29?

How many reasons can you think of for why the people of ancient Israel broke the Shemitah—and what did their breaking signify?

How did the breaking of the Shemitah turn it from a blessing to a curse?

Where in the Bible does it tell Israel what would happen if they broke the Shemitah? What would be the consequences of violating it?

How would the following effects of the Shemitah translate into modern economic terms?

- The nation's production dramatically decreases as its fields lay fallow.
- The nation's labor is greatly reduced or comes to a cessation.
- The fruits of the nation's fields are abandoned.
- Seed is not sown.
- Financial accounts are wiped away.

The Shemitah becomes a sign of judgment against a nation that does what?

The Shemitah and its last day, Elul 29, specifically affect what two realms of national life?

The Shemitah is based on a seven-year cycle. Between the first and second shakings of America in *The Harbinger*, how many years were there?

In what month did both shakings take place? In which week of that month?

The global economic crisis and collapse is dated from the fall of Northern Rock on September 13, 2007, to the greatest crash in American history, the peak of the global implosion, on September 29, 2008. What exact period began and ended on the same days?

The greatest stock market crash in American history took place on what day on the Hebrew biblical calendar?

What did that biblical day have to do with the economic or financial realm?

How did the economic collapse of 2008 follow the pattern of the Shemitah in outward form, the wiping away of financial accounts?

How many economic phenomena of the collapse and the Great Recession involve wiping away financial accounts, finances, numbers, credit, or debt?

If you start on the day of the greatest Wall Street crash in American history in 2008 and go back seven Hebrew biblical years, on what day do you end up?

What happened on that day seven years earlier in 2001?

Only one Elul 29 in seven years can end the Shemitah. On which Elul 29, out of seven years, was the date on which the greatest crash in American history took place in 2008? In 2001?

The Hebrew word *Shemitah* can be translated not only as "the release" or "the remission" but as "the "letting fall." How many different things can you think of that fell in the economic collapse? How might this be a warning to us concerning America's future?

■ *Spiritual Truths* ■

What factors that led Israel to break or stop observing the Shemitah are also now at work in America?

How can a nation's prosperity lead it away from its godly foundations?

How can a nation's turning away from God's Sabbath or rest lead to the worship of idols, materialism, and the serving of money?

What does the Shemitah as a sign of judgment say about the connection of a nation's relationship with God or turning away from God and its blessings such as prosperity?

■ *Mission to Apply This Week* ■

Have you lost or diminished your own Shemitah rest, daily quiet time with God?

What can you do this week to come back to or to create a Shemitah break or rest every day of your life from here on in so you can refocus on God, dwell in His presence, and receive His blessings? Write it down as your mission for the week in the space provided.

Take time now to commit this to God and pray for His help and anointing.

Seal this commitment in prayer (individually, in small groups, as a class, or congregationally).

Prepare for next week (groups only): This week read, go over, and explore the next chapter, "The Three Witnesses."

▨ *Write Down* ▨

1. Your thoughts, notes, and insights

2. What you believe the Lord is calling you to do

3. Your mission for the days ahead

Chapter 9

The THREE WITNESSES

The Law of Three Witnesses

T HERE IS A law in Scripture that a matter of judgment must be con-
firmed by two or three witnesses. Each witness must bear witness
consistent with the others.

> By the mouth of two or three witnesses the matter shall be
> established.
> —DEUTERONOMY 19:15

> By the mouth of two or three witnesses every word shall be
> established.
> —2 CORINTHIANS 13:1

What happens if this principle is applied to the realm of nations?
This study will explore what happens when the law of two or three wit-
nesses is applied to the realm of nations, and particularly to that of
America.

To set the stage, take note of the ancient vow of defiance and judgment in Isaiah 9:10:

The bricks have fallen,
But we will rebuild with hewn stone;
The sycamores have been cut down,
But we will plant cedars in their place.

The public proclamation of this vow connects America to ancient Israel, 9/11 with the opening warning strike concerning a nation's judgment, and America's post-9/11 response with the defiance of ancient Israel that led to the nation's destruction. It identifies America as the nation under judgment. In this, such a proclamation bears witness concerning judgment.

The Two Witnesses

- **The first witness:** September 12, 2001, Senate Majority Leader Tom Daschle proclaims the ancient vow of judgment on Capitol Hill the day after the calamity.

- **The second witness:** Three years later, on the anniversary of 9/11, vice-presidential candidate Senator John Edwards proclaims the same ancient vow and from the vow builds his entire speech.

Both witnesses unwittingly identified America with ancient Israel, 9/11 with Israel's opening strike of judgment, and America's response with the defiance of Israel that led to its destruction.

Each vowed, "We will rebuild." Each repeated ancient Israel's defiant declaration. Each unknowingly pronounced judgment on America. Each unwittingly bore witness.

The Third Witness

But the Scripture speaks of two or *three* witnesses. Could there be a third witness? There is. The third witness would confirm the connection of the ancient prophecy to today—and not just to 9/11 but also to the economic collapse seven years later. In so doing, this third witness served as a sign that the underlying course of judgment hadn't stopped but had progressed to a further stage.

This third witness was the new president of the United States, Barack Obama.

If one had to put the essence of the vow, its stones and sycamores, into modern English, it would be this: "We will rebuild. We will emerge stronger than before." One can find this very rendering in Bible commentaries on Isaiah 9:10.

On February 24, 2009, a month after his inauguration, President Obama appeared on Capitol Hill, the same place in which the first witness, the Senate majority leader, had first spoken the vow on the day after 9/11. His purpose was to address America's economic collapse. He quickly arrived at his central point, the pinnacle of his speech:

But while our economy may be weakened and our confidence shaken, though we are living through difficult and uncertain times, I want every American to know this:

We will rebuild.

We will recover.

And the United States of America will emerge stronger than before.[1]

"We Will Rebuild"

The words "we will rebuild" repeat Isaiah 9:10's ancient vow of defiance, but the context is, strangely, not the 9/11 attack but the economic crisis. In such a context, the vow appears unnatural. The first two witnesses were quoting Scripture but had no idea what they were saying. But the third witness doesn't even realize he's paraphrasing Scripture, the same that had twice been uttered by prominent Americans from the nation's capital.

The new president's oddly placed words bore witness that what had started with 9/11 had not ended but had continued in progression. Moreover, the words "we will rebuild," when uttered by President Obama, had no qualifier or limitation. They weren't tied to 9/11 or to the rebuilding of Ground Zero or New York.

The leaders of ancient Israel spoke of replacing clay bricks with hewn stone, and sycamores with cedars. In each case it was an example of a stronger object replacing a weaker. In view of the fact that they were responding to God's opening warning of judgment, they were, in effect, telling God, in defiance, that they would emerge from the crisis stronger than before. So now the president would publicly vow that the nation would emerge stronger than before.

A Comparison of Vows

Pete Souza / WhiteHouse.gov

Note the parallels that exist in the words spoken. When you take the words of a commentary on ancient Israel in Isaiah 9:10 and compare them to the president's vow on Capitol Hill, this is what happens:

- "They boasted that *they would rebuild* their devastated country..." (commentary: Israel's vow, emphasis added).
- "*We will rebuild*, we will recover" (the president's vow on Capitol Hill, emphasis added).
- "...*and make it stronger* and more glorious *than ever before*" (commentary: Israel's vow, emphasis added).
- "And the United States of America *will emerge stronger than before*" (president's vow, emphasis added).

The parallels continue with the president's other words. When ancient Israel uttered its rebellious vow, it was saying that it would decide its own future. According to one biblical commentary:

> The arrogant response demonstrates how stubborn and overconfident [they] were. *They thought they could determine their own destiny.*[2]

In like manner the president made this declaration:

The weight of this crisis *will not determine the destiny of this nation.*[3]

He then declared that the answer would be found in our nation's own strength, ingenuity, and efforts:

> The answers to our problems don't lie beyond our reach. They exist in our laboratories and universities; in our fields and our factories; in the imagination of our entrepreneurs and the pride of the hardest-working people on Earth.[4]

In other words, the president was saying in effect, "We will trust in our own strength and our own resources." This is exactly what the leaders of ancient Israel were saying when they spoke of hewn stones and erez trees.

The Words of Tom Daschle and the President

What the president vowed on Capitol Hill concerning the financial collapse, the second shaking, was virtually word for word what the Senate majority leader had vowed concerning 9/11, the first shaking, standing in the same place seven years earlier:

- "We will rebuild, and we will recover" (Tom Daschle, speaking of 9/11).
- "We will rebuild, and we will recover" (President Obama, speaking of the economic collapse).

The Prophetic Address

In the Bible a prophetic statement is often preceded by a prophetic address, identifying to whom the message is sent or directed. The vow of Isaiah 9:10 is preceded by this prophetic address:

> The LORD sent a word against Jacob,
> And it has fallen on Israel.
> All the people will know—

Ephraim and the inhabitant of Samaria...
"We will rebuild..."

—ISAIAH 9:8–10

The address identifies Jacob, Israel, Ephraim, and the inhabitants of Samaria as the ones to whom the prophecy is addressed. It speaks of the word "falling" on the nation and that *all the people will know* it. The word is for the entire nation so that all of its people will know it.

Now take note of the words spoken in both the president's speech and that of the Senate majority leader before the words of the vow:

> There is a passage in the Bible from Isaiah that I think speaks to *all of us* at times like this... "The bricks have fallen down, but *we will rebuild* with dressed stone..."[5]

> ...tonight I want *every American* to *know* this—We will rebuild...[6]

Note as with the first two witnesses, Senators Daschle and Edwards, the president was reciting the vow *on behalf of every American,* speaking *for* the nation. And, as did the first two witnesses, he was unwittingly bearing witness to America as a nation estranged from God and in defiance of His will.

Thus did the president of the United States join the economic collapse to Israel's ancient vow, as the first two witnesses joined 9/11 to those same words of defiance. Further, all three witnesses made the same proclamations in the same city, the nation's capital city, on the same hill, Capitol Hill, and in the same building, the one that housed the country's two highest representative bodies, each of which must confirm a law or proclamation in order to pass it, as with two witnesses.

The Harbingers in Cyberspace

One of the principles we've seen with the harbingers is that, one way or another, they become focal points. The tower at Ground Zero becomes the center of national attention. The hewn stone becomes the center of a ceremony. The fallen sycamore is put on display and commemorated in bronze. The erez tree becomes the center of a ceremony and is

103

likewise made into a symbol. The vow as proclaimed by Edwards opens his speech and becomes the center point and source for the rest of it. The vow as proclaimed by Daschle becomes the pinnacle of his speech, a speech that presents the nation's response to 9/11. In the case of the president's vow, the same dynamics begin to operate.

Once the speech was delivered, one set of words began to emerge. Of the thousands of words contained in Obama's speech, the words most often chosen by news services around the world were "We will rebuild." From the *New York Times* to *Al Jazeera*, they chose as their headlines the central defiant proclamation of Isaiah 9:10.

The ancient dynamic now operated in cyberspace. If one was to type into one's computer search engine the words "We will rebuild" before the speech, Isaiah 9:10 would appear on the screen in the first page of results. But as the American president spoke, his words began to replace the defiant words of America's leaders; his vow began to take the place of the ancient one.

Below is a sample of some of the many headlines that spread across the world on the Internet and in print in the wake of the president's speech:

Obama: "We will rebuild" (Associated Press)

Obama: "We will rebuild" (CBSNEWS)

Obama: "We will rebuild and emerge stronger than before" (THE GUARDIAN)

Obama Vows, "We will rebuild and recover" (The New York Times)

The ancient vow that had once brought destruction to Israel had now become, in the sight of all the world, the vow of America.

WEEK 9 EXPLORE *and* APPLY

Read chapter 18 of *The Harbinger.*

Watch or listen to the accompanying resource *The Three Witnesses* DVD or CD from *The Harbinger: The Full Revelation* eight-disc album.

Read Deuteronomy 19:15; 2 Corinthians 13:1; Isaiah 9:10; John 11:47–53.

■ *Explore* ■

What do you think the reason is for the law of two and three witnesses to establish a matter of judgment?

How can you see this law applied to the realm of nations, for instance, with regard to the judgment of Israel and Judah?

The high priest Caiaphas is recorded in John 11 as prophesying unwittingly. He doesn't realize what he's saying. How is this true also of all three witnesses who speak the ancient vow in one form or another?

Caiaphas spoke a double entendre—he said something that also meant something else. He intended to say one thing, but in the spiritual realm he said something altogether different and infinitely more profound. How did each of the three witnesses also speak in two different realms, one realm unwittingly, saying something infinitely more profound?

What did each of them intend to do? And what did each of them do without intending it?

Politicians and speechwriters are especially careful to measure every word to make sure it has no unintended consequence. Why then is it especially striking, especially in the case of the first two, that such words could be proclaimed by these men?

The Book of John records that Caiaphas said what he said not of his own accord but by virtue of his office. He was the high priest that year. He represented the nation. How is this principle of office also true of the three who spoke these words?

What was the significance of the city in the case of all three witnesses, and the hill, building, and chamber, in the case of the first and third witness? Why is that particular building most significant?

How significant were the words or paraphrase of Isaiah 9:10 in each speech? Explain.

Which one of the three closed his speech with the words of the ancient vow?

Which one of the three opened his speech with the words of the vow?

Which one of the three told his hearers that the words of the vow speak to all Americans?

Which one of the three based his entire speech on the ancient vow of Isaiah 9:10?

Which one of the three told his hearers that he wanted every American to know the vow?

How many of the three proclaimed the vow to members of the United States Congress?

Which one of the three was speaking not of 9/11 but of the economic collapse? He said almost word for word what was said concerning 9/11 the day after the attack. What significance could there be in that?

■ *Spiritual Truths* ■

Why is it significant that leaders make such proclamations?

What does it mean that leaders who may not even know God can say such prophetic utterances? What does it say about God's sovereignty?

What might be the significance of the fact that more than one of these vows were spoken in the same chamber, that of the House of Representatives, in a joint session of Congress?

What do you think the Lord could be saying in all this, the vow being proclaimed by three American leaders?

■ *Mission to Apply This Week* ■

Of the three witnesses, at least two knew they were quoting Scripture but had no idea what they were saying. The third didn't even realize he was quoting Scripture. But as believers, we are called to both witness and speak the Word of God. And to be true witnesses, we must be true to the Word of God—not using it for our own purposes, not bending it to match our lives but rather being used of it and conforming our lives to match the Word of God.

Take an honest look. Are there areas in your life that are not matching up with areas in the Word of God? What are they? Make it your mission this week to take specific steps to match up, conform, and move your life to match up with the Word of God. Write these steps down as your mission for the week in the space provided.

Take time now to commit this to God and pray for His help and anointing.

Seal this commitment in prayer (individually, in small groups, as a class, or congregationally).

Prepare for next week (groups only): This week read, go over, and explore the next chapter, "The Mystery Ground."

■ *Write Down* ■

1. Your thoughts, notes, and insights

2. What you believe the Lord is calling you to do

3. Your mission for the days ahead

Chapter 10

The MYSTERY GROUND

The Temple Mount

IN 586 BC calamity overtook the nation of Judah, and for the first time in its history, the Temple Mount lay in ruins. The Temple Mount was Israel's consecration ground, the place of prayer and communion with God. It was the site on which King Solomon had led Israel in prayer for its future on the day the nation had assumed its completed form. So when judgment came, the calamity, the destruction, had returned to the ground of consecration. This study explores the dynamics of the mystery ground, the message it holds for America, and the call to return. In a previous study we looked at the First Harbinger, the breach. As we noted, when Israel's ancient northern kingdom continued its centuries of apostasy in defiance of numerous warnings, God allowed a breach in its hedge of protection, letting the Assyrians launch an invasion of the land. A decade later, in 722 BC, when the northern kingdom failed to turn from its ways, God brought the Assyrians again, this time to destroy it and carry its people into exile. In 586 BC, following its own progression of apostasy, the southern kingdom, Judah, saw its own hedge of protection removed as Babylon destroyed the Temple in Jerusalem and exiled its people.

King Solomon and the Dedication

Built centuries earlier by King Solomon, the Temple Mount was the site of Israel's consecration to God. The Temple was also the focal point of Israel's national life. Its destruction revealed it as the focal point of judgment. When Solomon dedicated the Temple to God, he gathered the nation and its leaders to Jerusalem. Addressing the great throng, he recited God's record of covenant faithfulness. Offering up prayers for future generations, he also foresaw the nation's apostasy and its outcome, including the removal of God's blessing and favor, the withdrawal of His protective hedge, and the coming of calamity. Solomon's prayers were both prophetic and intercessory. His prayers foretold apostasy and resulting catastrophe and beseeched God for mercy and restoration for those generations yet to be born. After reciting in detail the tribulations, from famine and plagues to draughts and blight, that would come on Israel if they disobeyed God and refused to repent, Solomon prayed:

> When [your people] sin against you—for there is none who does
> not sin—and you...give them over to the enemy, who takes them
> captive...and if they turn back to you with all their heart and

soul...then...hear their prayer and their pleas, and uphold their cause. And forgive your people...

—2 Chronicles 6:36–39, niv

Thus, while the Temple's destruction was an immediate judgment, its ultimate purpose was mercy, as the Lord was calling the nation back to recall that the Temple Mount, the ground of its judgment, was also the ground of its original consecration by Solomon's generation, the foundation for all blessings.

The story of the Temple's dedication and destruction reveals a vital principle about a nation that dedicates itself to God and then turns from His ways despite repeated warnings:

The nation's ground of consecration will become the ground of its judgment.

America: The Day of Dedication

In the case of America, the day it reached its fully constituted form was not July 4, 1776, the day it declared independence from Britain, but April 30, 1789. On that day the nation's government was completed, as set forth in its Constitution, with the inauguration of its first president, George Washington. Taking his presidential oath, Washington placed his right hand on the same Bible that recorded Solomon's dedication of Israel to God and prophetic warnings and prayers for future generations in Israel. When Solomon dedicated the Temple to God, he did so in prayer and supplication (2 Chronicles 6). Washington did likewise:

> It would be peculiarly improper to omit in this first official act my fervent supplications to that Almighty Being who rules over the universe, who presides in the councils of nations, and whose providential aids can supply every human defect, that His benediction may consecrate to the liberties and happiness of the people of the United States a Government instituted by themselves for these essential purposes.[1]

And just as King Solomon was joined in prayer that day by the leaders and multitudes, "the whole assembly of Israel" (2 Chron. 6:3), so too was Washington as that seminal day in American history was designated as a day of prayer and dedication.

The Prophetic Warning

In the Bible days of dedication often become days prophetic words are spoken. When Jacob prayed over his sons, he also spoke prophetically of their future. Likewise, when the Messiah was dedicated as a child at the Temple, a prophetic word was spoken over Him. On the day of the Temple's dedication, King Solomon prayed prophetically for the nation's future, its coming apostasy and judgment. So too on the day the American nation-state and government came into existence, a prophetic word was spoken.

In the first ever presidential address, Washington gave a prophetic warning to the nation:

> The propitious smiles of Heaven can never be expected on a nation that disregards the eternal rules of order and right which Heaven itself hath ordained.[2]

What was Washington saying? It was simply this: If America upholds God's eternal standards of righteousness she will be blessed with His protection and prosperity. But if America should ever disregard God's eternal standards of righteousness, if she should ever depart from His ways, His blessings would be withdrawn from the land.

The American Mystery Ground

Photo by Andrea Booher/FEMA

After Washington finished his speech, the first completed government of the United States embarked on its first official act. It was not to pass a bill or argue legislation; it was to pray. The entire government, including the Senate and House of Representatives, went on foot to the place appointed for prayer.

The site on which America's future was dedicated to God in prayer could be called the nation's dedication ground or consecration ground. And where was it? It took place in the nation's capital. But the capital of America on that first inaugural day was not Washington DC or Philadelphia. America's first capital was New York City. Where exactly was America dedicated to God? What exactly is America's consecration ground?

America's consecration ground is Ground Zero.

They gathered to commit America's future to God at the corner of Ground Zero. In fact, the very ground on which the twin towers stood was church land. They dedicated America's future to God in a little stone building, St. Paul's Chapel, which still stands there to this day.

And it was on there, on America's consecration ground, that the Sixth Harbinger, the Sycamore, had grown. It was into that soil that the Erez Tree was planted in place of the fallen tree.

Thus, on the day that America's foundation was laid and the nation's future committed to God's "holy protection," it happened at precisely the place where, on 9/11, His holy protection was, in part, withdrawn.

The Cracked Foundation

It was in Federal Hall, New York City, that the American nation as we know it came into existence. It was on its balcony where Washington was sworn in as the nation's first president. It was there in its chamber where Washington gave that prophetic warning. Today, in New York City, on Wall Street, facing the New York Stock Exchange, stands a statue of Washington. The inscription on the pedestal reads as follows:

> On this site in Federal Hall, April 30, 1789, George Washington took
> the Oath as the First President of the United States of America.[3]

On that founding day, the two sites, Federal Hall and St. Paul's Chapel (Ground Zero), were joined together. On September 11, 2001, the two sites were joined together again. When the twin towers fell, a shock wave moved from Ground Zero to Federal Hall, putting a crack in its foundation—in America's foundation—the place where Washington's

115

prophetic warning was spoken as to what would happen if the nation ever turned away from God.

Washington had warned that the nation would witness its blessings removed. The nation was now witnessing those blessings removed, one by one, from its physical security and later its economic prosperity. From the devastation of Ground Zero at St. Paul's, the nation's ground of consecration, to the crash of the New York Stock Exchange at Federal Hall, the site of the foundation where Washington's words were spoken, the warning was coming true.

"The Miracle of 9/11" and the Purpose of the Harbingers

All around Ground Zero every building was either destroyed or ruined—all except for one. One was protected. It was called "the miracle of 9/11." What was it? It was St. Paul's Chapel, the little stone building in which America was dedicated to God. And why was it protected? There was an object that absorbed the force of the calamity and protected the church. What was it? It was the harbinger, the Sycamore of Ground Zero, the Sixth Harbinger, that shielded the church both from the force of the implosion and the flying wreckage of the falling towers.

In this, the purpose of the harbingers and the message of *The Harbinger*, is revealed. This Sixth Harbinger protected the place where America's future was dedicated to God. The point is not to condemn a nation to judgment but to save it. If there were no hope, there would be no harbingers. The point of warning is hope.

The message of the "mystery ground," as with the Temple Mount in ancient Israel, was not only that the nation's consecration to God had been broken. It was also a message of return—the voice of God calling the nation to return from where it had fallen—to return to Him.

The place where the first American government had once prayed for its future now became the center not only of calamity but also of the relief efforts made in the wake of that calamity. Without knowing quite why, multitudes were drawn there. In the wake of 9/11 the nation's attention and focus had returned to the ground on which its future had once been consecrated to God.

WEEK 10 EXPLORE *and* APPLY

Read chapter 19 of *The Harbinger*.

Watch or listen to the accompanying resource *The Mystery Ground* DVD or CD from *The Harbinger: The Full Revelation* eight-disc album.

Read 2 Chronicles 5:1–5; 6:3–4; 6:15; 6:28–30; 36:11–19.

▦ *Explore* ▦

What was the significance of the Temple to ancient Israel?

How was the Temple both the place of Israel's consecration to God and its judgment by God?

At the Temple's dedication, what did King Solomon foretell?

At its dedication, how did Solomon intercede for Israel?

How was the Temple's destruction both an act of judgment and mercy?

When the Temple was finished and dedicated, the nation of Israel was complete, having assumed its completed form. When was America's form as a nation completed?

How many parallels can you find between Israel's dedication day and America's?

What was the prophetic warning that America's first president gave to the nation on that first and critical day?

What are the "smiles of Heaven"?

What did George Washington mean when he spoke of a nation disregarding the eternal rules of right and order "which Heaven itself hath ordained"? What are those eternal rules?

How is this coming true in our day—a nation disregarding the eternal rules of heaven?

How are we seeing the smiles of heaven disappearing?

What was the first act of the first fully formed American government?

On America's first day as a fully formed nation, what was America's capital city where this all took place?

Where was America's future on this day consecrated to God? What is the nation's consecration ground?

What structures stood on the adjoining field of St. Paul's Chapel, also part of the church's land?

We discussed the ancient principle of calamity returning to a nation's ground of consecration. How did this principle manifest on September 11, 2001?

What harbingers manifested on America's consecration ground?

On 9/11 a shock wave went forth from Ground Zero and struck Federal Hall. For what is Federal Hall significant? (You may have more than one answer to this.)

What object in New York City marks what happened at Federal Hall in 1789?

The shock wave of 9/11 put a crack in Federal Hall, the nation's foundation. What might such a thing signify?

What was "the miracle of 9/11"? And what might that signify?

What object is believed to have caused "the miracle of 9/11"? And why is that object significant?

■ *Spiritual Truths* ■

The Harbinger protected and saved the place where America was consecrated to God. What insight into the purpose of the harbingers does this give us?

In Hebrew the word for "repentance" is *teshuvah*, and it means both repentance and return. The events of 9/11 caused America's focus to return to the place where America was dedicated to God at its beginning—a return to the foundation. What kind of return would this signify, and what might the call of God be saying to America?

◼ *Mission to Apply This Week* ◼

Is there a "place" in God, a higher ground where you once stood, a time when you were closer to Him, or more in His Word or in prayer, more pure of heart, or a time when He was more your "first love" than now?

Is God calling you to return in some way to your first love, to the simplicity of your faith in Him, and to the joy of His love and presence?

If so, what steps can you take this week to begin your journey to where you need to be in the Lord? Write them down in the space provided, and make them your mission for this week.

Take time now to commit this to God and pray for His help and anointing.

Seal this commitment in prayer (individually, in small groups, as a class, or congregationally).

Prepare for next week (groups only): This week read, go over, and explore the next chapter, "What Lies Ahead?"

▨ *Write Down* ▨

1. Your thoughts, notes, and insights

2. What you believe the Lord is calling you to do

3. Your mission for the days ahead

Chapter 11

WHAT LIES AHEAD?

What Happened to Ancient Israel

W HAT HAPPENS WHEN a nation ignores the warnings of God
and the call to return? What happened to ancient Israel?
What happens to nations that return to God? What about America?
What does the future hold? This chapter explores the biblical principles
and patterns concerning the judgment or redemption of nations and
peoples and the revelation it holds for America.

As we have seen, when the people of Israel's northern kingdom fell
into apostasy, God repeatedly called them to return. The very words of
the Torah, spoken through Moses to their ancestors in Leviticus 26 and
Deuteronomy 28, were His first call and His foretelling future calamity
if they failed to repent. When they ignored those words, God sent His
prophets to confront the nation face-to-face with its transgressions.

Even then the people and their leaders refused to listen, hardening their hearts to His message and persecuting the messengers. God finally allowed Israel's enemies to breach His protective hedge around the nation, causing significant damage.

Yet as we saw, the damage was limited. Even in judgment God was calling the nation to wake up, turn from its self-destructive course, and be reconciled to Him.

Isaiah 9:10 was the nation's defiant answer to God's final call. Verse 11 describes the beginning of the tragic consequences of that defiance, the nation's progression to judgment:

> Therefore the LORD shall set up the adversaries of Rezin against him and spur his enemies on.

The answer continues in the verses that follow:

> And they shall devour Israel with an open mouth.
> For all this His anger is not turned away,
> But His hand is stretched out still...
> The land is burned up....
> What will you do in the day of punishment,
> And in the desolation which will come from afar?
> To whom will you flee for help?
> —ISAIAH 9:12, 19; 10:3

Thus, Isaiah 9:10 leads to a prophecy of national destruction, fulfilled when the Assyrians returned, laid siege for three years, and destroyed the northern kingdom in 722 BC and exiled its people.

What Lies Ahead for America

We have seen in America's story the same patterns of apostasy, initial warnings, and a further warning through the limited calamity of 9/11. We have seen how all Nine Harbingers of Israel's coming judgment, including all that is contained in Isaiah 9:10, have been manifested in America. We have also seen how, in the years since 9/11, America, like ancient Israel, failed to return to God's ways but responded in defiance, and how seven years later there came a second shaking of the nation.

If America continues on its course away from and in defiance of God, what lies ahead?

The Bible reveals several patterns of judgment but involving a consistent course. The nation's blessings are removed by means of the sword (i.e., war), destruction, violence, or division. The pattern also involves famine (i.e., lack, want, deprivation, the removal of prosperity, impoverishment). Judgment can involve natural disaster, man-made disaster, terrorism, internal division, the collapse of a nation's infrastructure, decline, and fall.

In the case of a nation so blessed as has been America, it would certainly involve the removal of these blessings. And in the case of a nation given the position of "head of nations" economically, financially, culturally, politically, and militarily, it would also involve the removal of this crown. Thus, if America does not turn back to God, we can likely anticipate the end of history's American age.

Judgment or Redemption?

But is judgment inevitable? What cases do we see in the Bible of a nation hanging in the balance?

We have the case of Sodom, in which not even ten righteous people could be found. The result was destruction.

A nation can partially turn back to God through the influence of godly leaders, as the southern kingdom of Judah did under King Josiah, experiencing a revival during their rule, only to backslide over the next generation and face judgment. In that case judgment was postponed.

Finally, a nation can turn completely to God in repentance, as Nineveh did after the warnings of the prophet Jonah, and avoid judgment for generations to come. In that case the judgment was turned back, and the city was saved.

Between a future of judgment or revival, there is another possibility. There can be both. Sometimes revival only comes through judgment, through shaking, through loss. Most people come to the Lord through such shaking and loss, or some kind of crisis, external or internal. So it is with nations. After 9/11 people flocked to houses of worship. It looked as if there could be a national revival. But the movement was short-lived. There was no real repentance, no changing of course. And without repentance, there can be no revival.

But what happened in those first few weeks after 9/11 shows the connection between calamity or shaking and revival. It is often only through such calamity and shaking that people return to the Lord and to their first love. So there is possibility also for a dual picture: judgment concerning the ungodliness of American mainstream culture but revival for those who in the midst turn to God in repentance.

End-Time Prophecy

Which course will America follow? A look at end-time prophecy may provide some answers.

One of the key signs that we have entered the period known biblically as the end times is the miraculous return of the Jewish people to their land, following twenty centuries of exile—all in accordance with biblical prophecy.

> For I will take you from among the nations, gather you out of all countries, and bring you into your own land.
> —Ezekiel 36:24

> Behold, O My people, I will open your graves and…bring you into the land of Israel.
> —Ezekiel 37:12

As the Bible foretells, the reborn nation of Israel and the city of Jerusalem will be the center of controversy (Zech. 12). Besides Israel returning as a nation, a further sign of the end times will be the rise of a one-world government, the most powerful in history. It will be associated with a godless ruler, alluded to in the Book of Daniel and described more fully in the Book of Revelation. Called "the beast," he is worshipped by the world, blasphemes God, wars against God's people, and conquers the nations through war and seduction (Rev. 13:4–8).

As the Book of Zechariah foretells, Israel will eventually be attacked by all nations. As Revelation 16 relates, it is the one-world ruler who gathers them against her. As both Zechariah and Revelation state, God will, through the return of the Messiah, destroy this final attempt to wipe out Israel and set up His kingdom in Jerusalem.

The Missing Superpower

All this leads up to the question: Where is America in all these prophecies? The answer is that there is no clear reference to America in end-time prophecy. Moreover, not a word is said in these end-times prophecies about Israel's most powerful human ally rescuing Israel. It is God who literally does so in the end.

Thus between where we are now and where the world is at the end of the age, there is a gap and a question: How do we go from the American age where America stands preeminent among nations, to a post-American age as revealed in end-time prophecy? Something has to happen.

The Harbinger fills in the gaps between where we are and what is yet to come.

At the same time, even though the overall direction of American culture points to a continued progression of moral descent, apostasy, shaking, and judgment, we cannot underestimate the power of prayer and the Lord's Spirit. And even in the midst of apostasy, shaking, and judgment there can be true revival among those who seek Him.

WEEK 11 EXPLORE *and* APPLY

Read chapter 20 of *The Harbinger*.

Read Isaiah 9:10–10:3; Ezekiel 36:24; 37:12; Zechariah 12; Revelation 13:4–8.

▪ *Explore* ▪

How did ancient Israel ultimately respond to God's repeated calls to turn from her sins?

What were the consequences of ancient Israel's failure to repent and return?

Why did the people fail to respond to the Nine Harbingers and other warnings and never return to God?

In the case of Sodom, what was the condition God gave for the city to be spared judgment?

What does this say about the heart and will of God?

In the case of Judah, her judgment was decreed but was then held back, postponed, delayed. Because of what or whom?

What does that reveal?

In the case of Nineveh, was there any hope given in the warning of the prophet Jonah?

Then why was there salvation?

What was it that the people of Nineveh did that the others did not?

What is significant about the salvation of Nineveh with regard to the people who inhabited it (and linked to Isaiah 9:10)?

After God judged ancient Israel, was He through with His people?

What is the evidence from Scripture that He was not through with His people?

What does the return of the Jewish people to the land of Israel say about God's ancient covenant with His people?

What should our stance as a nation be toward Israel and its people?

What does it say about His faithfulness to believers today?

What are some of the key signs of the end times according to biblical prophecy that are being fulfilled today?

What does the Bible say about America in the end times? What does this mean?

If America is not mentioned in biblical end-times prophecies, how is there still hope for this nation?

How can judgment come to a nation such as America?

How can we be safe?

What is the Hebrew word for safety or salvation? And what does this have to do with the gospel?

■ *Spiritual Truths* ■

How can our own generation in modern America avoid the fate of ancient Israel?

How does God's eternal, unconditional love for Israel in spite of her sins relate to our own lives and walk with Him as individual believers?

■ *Mission to Apply This Week* ■

In view of the signs of the time and the lateness of the hour, what changes should this cause in the way you live? If you knew you only had a limited time left, maybe even one week, how would you change things in your life, especially in the following areas?

- Your living with, dealing with—or not dealing with—sin
- Your non-responsiveness to God's calling for you to rise higher in Him
- The things you've put off doing but which you know you need to do
- Your relationships, unforgiveness, walls, unresolved areas
- Sharing the gospel with the unsaved
- Your relationship and time with God

What specific steps can you take this week to start changing your life? Write them down in the space provided on the next page. This is your mission for the week.

Take time now to commit this to God and pray for His help and anointing.

Seal this commitment in prayer (individually, in small groups, as a class, or congregationally).

NOTE: Leader, this could be a good time for a presentation and call to salvation.

Prepare for next week (groups only): This week read, go over, and explore the next chapter, "The Call."

▨ *Write Down* ▨

1. Your thoughts, notes, and insights

2. What you believe the Lord is calling you to do

3. Your mission for the days ahead

Chapter 12

The CALL

If My People

IS THERE HOPE?

Consider this. If there were no hope, there would be no harbingers. What is the point of warning if there's no hope of responding to that warning? If there are harbingers, there is hope.

Even the fact that *The Harbinger* has become a national best seller, spreading across the nation, can be taken the same way. If there were no hope, what would be the point?

Then if there is hope, what is it?

Is there a scripture linked to the mystery ground that, though given to Israel, speaks and calls to us now and provides the answer? And does each of us have a part in all of this? And if so, what is that part? This study explores the hope, the chance, the keys for revival, and the very concrete part we all have in that hope and in being an agent for redemption.

In a prior study we saw the connection between Israel's dedication ground and America's. We saw King Solomon's prayer to God, one of prophecy about apostasy and judgment but also one of intercession for future generations. Solomon beseeched the Lord to show mercy and favor on those future generations who, having experiencing calamity due to their repeatedly turning from God and their refusals to turn back, would come to their senses and repent.

When the dedication of the Temple Mount was completed, God answered King Solomon's prayer in this way:

> If My people who are called by My name will humble themselves, and pray and seek My face, and turn from their wicked ways, then I will hear from heaven, and will forgive their sin and heal their land.
>
> —2 Chronicles 7:14

Who are "My people"? As given to Solomon, this can refer both to the nation of Israel as a whole and specifically those within the nation who know the Lord. It's the call of God for a nation, once dedicated to His purposes but now defying His will, to return.

With the connection we've already seen between Israel's dedication ground and America's, as well as the manifestation of all Nine Harbingers in America, we can take it as well as a call to America. Even without this connection, it lays a very sure foundation that in the face of judgment God's people are called to pray, to seek, and to repent—and God will hear, forgive, and heal.

The Keys to Redemption and Revival

If My people who are called by My name *will humble themselves...*

This means we must come before God with no claims, no rights, no self-righteousness, no standing, no goodness of our own, nothing but the hope of His mercy. It means we must abandon any notion and any reliance on our own power, our own righteousness, or our own sufficiency and acknowledge God's all-sufficient power.

And *pray...*

America was founded on prayer. Thus the removal of prayer from its public life was a key part of its falling away from its foundation in God. A nation that rejects prayer will find itself desperately needing it. The calamity of 9/11 returned America to its ground of consecration. The nation was being called to return to God in prayer.

And *seek My face...*

To seek God's face is to desire His presence and His will above all else. It requires spending time turned away from everything else but His presence.

And *turn from their wicked ways...*

To "turn from wicked ways" means to repent, to change your mind completely about sin. America must face the magnitude of our moral and spiritual descent. We must face the enormity of the degrading of our culture. We must face our downward spiral into ever-deeper levels of defiance and immorality. We must face the proliferation of our idols, from carnality and impurity to greed and materialism. We must face our love of vanity and our drive toward self-obsession. We must face our cruel mockery of the pure and our mass sacrifice of the innocent and helpless.

My People = Us

Revival does not begin with government, with culture, with politics, with economics, or with anything else. Revival begins with the people of God and then touches every area of life. If not us, who? If not here, where? And if not now, when? Revival must begin with us, it must begin here, and it must begin now.

The call is to the people of God; the call is to us.

We are the ones being called to repent of our apathy and our complacency. We must repent for all of our compromises with the darkness. God is calling us to repent of our own sins, sins of *omission*—that which we have been called to do but have not done—and sins of *com-mission*—that which we have done, that which we do but have been called to stop. We ourselves must repent of failing to tear down the high places, the idols of our own hearts, for indulging in secret sins, sins of the flesh, sins of the mind, sins of the heart, for partaking in the sins of our culture that stand under the judgment of God. We ourselves must repent of withholding the light of the gospel from the unsaved, for not sharing His Word. We ourselves must repent of not standing against what is wrong and for what is right, for seeking our own comfort instead of His righteousness. We ourselves must repent of failing to rise to the high calling that God has given us and to which the Spirit has called us continually.

And if believers repent and lead the nation in repentance, then there is a promise:

> I will hear from heaven, and will forgive their sin and heal their land.

Revivals Past... and Future?

Will America repent and be revived?

As noted in earlier chapters, the landscape of our history is dotted with great revivals, starting with the very first colonists. Revivals in Britain led to the Pilgrims and Puritans arriving on America's shores, becoming the forerunners of the nation.

America's first great homegrown revival, referred to as The Great Awakening, sowed the seeds in the 1740s for the emerging of a brand-new nation. Revivals in the 1800s unleashed the abolitionist movement that stirred the nation's conscience against slavery. Revivals of the past century turned millions of baby boomers, those from a generation that had once declared God dead, into godly people of faith who continue to stand against America's moral and spiritual decline.

Judgment, Salvation, and the Day We Stand Before Him

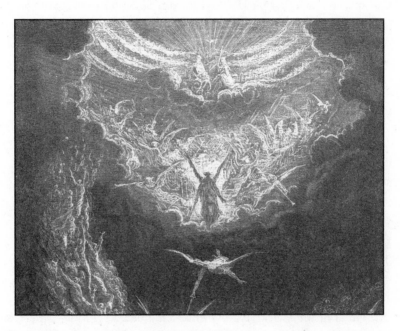

Every story of national revival begins with repentance and prayer.

But a nation's repentance rests on the repentance of individuals within it. Since nations are temporal and souls are eternal, individual repentance remains paramount.

Within even the purest of hearts evil is real. The Bible says that there are none who are righteous. All have fallen. All must repent. Even the seemingly best human beings are closer to the most wicked of people than they are to the perfect goodness of the God who created them.

Every sin and every evil will be judged. Every soul that is joined to sin stands in danger of judgment. The final judgment will be eternal separation from God—hell. In the end there are only two roads, heaven or hell. But the Bible declares in John 3:16 that "God so loved the world that He gave His only begotten Son, that whoever would believe in Him would not perish but have everlasting life." The greatest love we can ever know is that of the God who gave His own Son, His own life, to stand in our place, to receive our judgment, that we would not be judged but saved, that we would have eternal life. That, in a nutshell, is the gospel.

135

The word *Yeshua* in Hebrew means "salvation." From the same root word comes the name *Jesus*. Jesus is salvation and remains the answer. The gospel message is that He died for our sins and rose again that we might be saved.

The Sign Amidst the Ruins

In the ruins of the World Trade Center emerged a symbol—a perfectly formed, twenty-foot-high cross, shaped not by human hands but by the force of the 9/11 calamity. It was called the Cross of Ground Zero. This sign calls not only the nation but also each individual to turn from the path of judgment and embrace repentance and redemption from a God who is love. It's a call to personal redemption by accepting God's atoning sacrifice in Yeshua, who bore an infinite judgment so that each person who accepts Him can enjoy God's infinite mercy. It's a call to cross over from a path leading to death to one leading to a second birth, from a God who is both gift and gift-giver of new life. It is a call to become wedded to the One who desires to become the Bridegroom of our soul.

Salvation isn't about your religion. Whether you are Catholic, Protestant, Jewish, Muslim, Hindu, or anything else—it doesn't matter. You cannot be born into heaven; you must be born again. God is Spirit. The only way to be His child is to be born of the Spirit. So Jesus Himself said, "You must be born again" (John 3:7). The Bible is very clear. There is no way to enter heaven, there is no way to be saved, unless you are born again. It doesn't matter how good or bad you have been or how far away from God you are; the love of God reaches out to all. The Lord is calling.

One day we will all stand before God on the Day of Judgment. If we are not born again, we stand with our sins and enter eternal judgment. If we are born again, we stand in forgiveness, and we enter into eternal life—heaven. The only time we have to prepare for that day is now. How much time do we have? How far away are we from that day? One heartbeat. That's all. Every moment of our lives is hanging on one heartbeat. We don't know when the last one will come. That is why the Bible says, "Now is the day of salvation" (2 Cor. 6:2).

The Call

If you are not born again, now is the time to become so and to get right with God.

If you have known God but haven't been living it, you've been out of His perfect will; now is the time to get right with God.

If there is anything in your life that needs to be removed or anything not in your life that needs to come in, now is the time to come to God and begin.

And perhaps God is simply calling you to return to your first love, to on-fire devotion to Him, to higher ground, to revival; now is the time to consecrate your heart and life to doing it.

The voice of God is calling.

Now is the time to get right with Him.

WEEK 12 EXPLORE *and* APPLY

Read chapters 21 and 22 of *The Harbinger*.

Watch or listen to the accompanying resource *If My People* DVD or CD from the eight-disc set.

Read 2 Chronicles 7:14.

■ *Your Final Exploration and Mission* ■

Can there be revival in America?

Can prayer change history?

How does revival come? Through whom? What people specifically?

Does God use people in bringing revival?

The priests of Israel were called to bring the nation to God. But before they could do that, they had to get their own lives right with God, to confess their sins, and enter His presence. In the same way we cannot lead others to repentance of their sins if we ourselves are not repenting of our sins; we cannot lead others to revival if we ourselves are not living in revival. Nor can we help lead others into God's presence if we ourselves are not entering into His presence.

The last mission is for you to do whatever is necessary to fulfill God's purposes, to be a vessel for revival—individually, as a group, a Bible study, a class, a congregation.

This final week will be devoted to fulfilling the call of God; to a special time of coming into God's presence in prayer, intercession, worship, in seeking God's face, and consecrating ourselves to Him and His purposes; to higher ground; to increased devotion, commitment, and power; to serving, following, and loving Him as never before.

▨ *To Prepare:* ▨

If you are doing an individual study of this book, make a copy of the sheet on the next page for yourself and fill out the top section as you feel led. Then pray and ask God to seal this commitment and begin to fulfill it.

If you are in a group, make a copy for each person and go through it with everyone, giving time to do it together with everyone filling out the top part individually as they feel led. For the group commitment, the leader can let everyone know what to write as you all fill it out together. Then everyone will keep their own copy of the commitment.

If you have any in your group who may not be saved, take this time to present a call to salvation.

Ask everyone to lift up their commitment sheets together and pray for God to seal this commitment and to begin fulfilling it. Encourage everyone to prepare for next time, which will be the final study week. (They should bring their sheets next week.)

COMMITMENT SHEET FOR THE LORD'S PURPOSES

Repentance: What is God calling me to remove from my life once and for all? What action can I take this week to begin doing it? _____

_____

Higher Calling: What new thing is God calling me to now, into my life, that is not now there? What action can I take this week to begin doing it? _____

_____

Prayer: As my new commitment to increased time with God in daily prayer and quiet time, I will commit to: _____

_____

God's Word: As my new commitment to increased applying of God's Word every day, I will commit to: _____

_____

The Gospel: As my new commitment to increased spreading the Word, the gospel, of salvation to the lost continually, I will commit to: _____

_____

Overall: As my new commitment to rising to higher ground in God, to increased commitment and consecration to Him in every way, to seeking Him, and to becoming a holy vessel of His purposes and revival, I will commit to (list specific actions you will begin this week):

_____

_____

I also commit to interceding for others and praying for revival, for the lost, and for this nation. _____

_____

GROUP/CLASS/OR CONGREGATIONAL AGREEMENT

What can we do as a group to help bring about revival? We agree together to:

_____

_____

Prayer: We commit to prayer by: _____

_____

Evangelism: We commit to evangelism and sharing the gospel by: _____

_____

Other: We commit to: _____

_____

Bring this sheet to the final session/class.

Chapter 13

ANSWERING *the* CALL

W E HAVE GONE through the mysteries, revelations, message, and call of *The Harbinger.* The purpose of it all is for God's mercy, redemption, salvation, and revival. It is not only to learn about the calling of God for salvation and revival but also to be part of the answer.

So this finale is devoted to actually coming into God's presence in worship, in prayer, in intercession for revival and for America, in personal commitment and consecration, and group dedication. *Do great things for the Lord for such a time as this!*

Individuals

If you have been studying this book as an individual, take this time to be in God's presence. You can follow the suggestions for a "Special Time in God's Presence" in this chapter or simply look over your commitment sheet and create a prayer list of people you know (family, friends, neighbors, coworkers, congregation members, and so on). Then pray for yourself, the people on your list, and finally for our nation.

Groups

If you are leading a small group or congregation through this study, ask your group to look over their commitment sheets. If some have forgotten them, remind them of what you've committed to. Next, let everyone know what you're going to do and how your group is going to pray. Start by praying for yourselves and then your group, congregation, or community and finally for the nation. You as the leader can lead in prayer, and if led, others can lead out at different points. But the main thing is to keep the flow of prayer moving, directing it to the new things to be prayed for. Feel free to use the following suggestions for a "Special Time in God's Presence."

Special Time in God's Presence

- Enter into God's presence and spend time lifting up the Lord.

- Read 2 Chronicles 7:14 again and really focus on what it's saying: humble yourself, seek His face, and turn from sinful ways by confessing sin, repenting of sin, and committing to Him.

- Have everyone look at their commitment sheets, allowing each individual time to pray for the things they've committed to do at the top of the sheet. Pray for repentance (to renounce, remove from our lives that which has to go), a higher calling (to take up, embrace to whatever God is calling us to, and to apply it to our lives), an increased commitment to prayer, to follow or apply the Word every day, to share the gospel with the unsaved, and to overall consecration.

- Then lift up the commitment sheets and pray corporately for the group commitments on the sheets, for group prayer, group evangelism, and other commitments. Pray for consecration (sealing) of everyone.

- Then pray for America. Intercede for our nation's sins, cry out for mercy, pray for revival from one coast to the other. Call out states, regions, cities, people groups, leaders, and for anything else you are led to pray for, and pray for God to have His way.

- Close with a time of sealing these commitments to God, asking for His power to fulfill them.

- Finish with a time of worship.

■ SECTION II ■
SPECIAL FEATURES

א ת

Chapter 14

The HARBINGER:
The STORY *and the* PEOPLE

A JOURNALIST, NOURIEL KAPLAN, appears in the office of Ana Goren, an executive in media, telling her that he has a mystery to reveal, a mystery that goes back to ancient times and that holds the secret to America's future.

He reveals to her what appears to be an ancient clay seal and begins to tell his account of his encounters with a mysterious man he simply refers to as "the prophet." The encounters take place in various places in New York City, Washington DC, and beyond, each encounter unannounced, unplanned for, as if just happening to happen or preordained.

Each encounter centers around a clay seal given to Nouriel by the prophet. There are nine altogether. Each seal contains a mystery that Nouriel must uncover. Each mystery goes back to ancient times and yet reveals exactly what is happening to America.

The mysteries lie behind everything from 9/11 to the collapse of the American economy and what lies ahead in the nation's future. Each mystery is a puzzle piece in a still larger revelation that links together the Nine Harbingers of judgment that appeared in the last days of ancient Israel before its destruction and that are now reappearing on American soil.

The mystery continues to build until the revealing of the last seal and the final mystery, which brings it all home to *The Harbinger* end...and beginning.

Key People in the Story

Nouriel Kaplan

Nouriel is a writer, a journalist, Jewish American, secular. He lives in New York and is in conflict with his life's course. He feels as if what he does has little meaning, that there should be more. As a journalist and by nature, he's skeptical, sometimes irreverent, but when he sees something that defies natural explanation or doesn't fit into his frame of reference, he is inquisitive to seek it out. When Nouriel receives an unexpected package in the mail, he embarks on a journey that will irreversibly change his course and his life.

Ana Goren

Ana is an executive in media, in the publishing industry, with main offices in midtown New York City; she is intelligent, naturally skeptical, sometimes cynical, jaded, tough, sometimes impatient, and yet caring. Beneath the generally tough exterior she is sincere and open to what she doesn't know, even seeking. When, one day, a man appears in her office with an ancient object, an unbelievable story, and a mystery he claims holds the secret of America's future, she is, at first, skeptical and ready to dismiss him. But as he continues to speak, her skepticism begins to make way for a curiosity and an openness that will cause her to set aside everything else to pursue it.

"The prophet"

This is the most mysterious of the characters in *The Harbinger*. He never gives his name, where he lives, or any means of contact. He is somewhat thin, with dark hair, Mediterranean or Middle Eastern looking, with a closely cropped beard. He never reveals where he comes from or where he's going. He never calls himself a prophet or gives himself any title. He is both enigmatic and revealing, drawing in and leading Nouriel further along the course of the mystery. There is an otherness, a distinct separateness about him, as if in his circumstances but not fully of them, and yet he is very much aware of his surroundings and the world. Mysterious, the prophet is also compassionate toward Nouriel and often manifests a distinct sense of humor.

Key Biblical Figures
in *The Harbinger*

Isaiah: The prophet behind the harbingers

Hebrew: *Yishaiyahu,* meaning "God is salvation"

It is Isaiah's prophecy concerning ancient Israel that forms the backdrop of *The Harbinger* and the key to the Nine Harbingers reappearing in America.

Isaiah prophesied in the eighth century BC, during the reigns of King Uzziah, Jotham, Ahaz, and Hezekiah, who ruled over the southern kingdom of Judah. It was a time of great geopolitical unrest. It was during this time that the shadow of the Assyrian Empire expanded to threaten both the northern kingdom of Samaria and the southern kingdom of Judah. It was against this backdrop that Isaiah gave his prophecy concerning the arrogant defiance of the northern kingdom and its ultimate destruction.

Isaiah is considered to be the greatest of the Hebrew prophets, and the Book of Isaiah, the greatest prophetic book of Hebrew prophecy. The Book of Isaiah includes the prophecy of Messiah's birth (in the same chapter as Isaiah 9:10), the prophecy of Messiah's suffering and death (Isaiah 53), and, in the latter chapters, several glimpses into the Messianic kingdom.

Jeremiah: The weeping prophet of judgment

Hebrew: *Yirmayahu*, meaning "God has raised up"

The Harbinger contains more than one quote from the Book of Jeremiah. Known as "the weeping prophet," Jeremiah is the epitome of a prophet living in the days of judgment. Near the end of *The Harbinger*, the examples of Jeremiah and Baruch, the prophet's scribe, appear as a prototype for the last revelation.

Jeremiah ministered in the last days of the kingdom of Judah. Beginning his ministry in the reign of King Josiah, Jeremiah revealed the sins of his countrymen and warned the nation of coming judgment. For this he was hated, persecuted, plotted against, and thrown into prison.

The warnings of Jeremiah came true in 586 BC when the kingdom of Judah and the city of Jerusalem were destroyed by the armies of Babylon.

Baruch: The scribe

Hebrew: *Baruch*, meaning "blessed"

Baruch provides a key puzzle piece to the final mystery. He stands as a representative of the scribes of Israel. Baruch was a *sofer,* one who committed the oral word to parchment, a scribe, particularly, the scribe of the prophet Jeremiah. It was Baruch who first committed Jeremiah's prophecy to written form, the first version of the Book of Jeremiah.

When, because of King Jehoiakim's persecution, Jeremiah went into hiding, he instructed Baruch to publicly read his prophecies to warn the people gathered in the Temple courts. At great risk to himself Baruch carried out the prophet's orders.

Caiaphas: The prophesying anti-prophet

Hebrew: *Kayafah*, meaning "a depression"

Caiaphas appears in *The Harbinger* as an example of how one who would not be called a prophet can unwittingly utter a prophetic word. Yosef Bar Kayafah, or Joseph Caiaphas, was high priest of Israel from the years AD 18 to 36, holding the office longer than any other man in New Testament history. Behind Caiaphas' reign was the figure of Annas, who had his five sons appointed to the same position of high priest at different times. Caiaphas, by marrying Annas' daughter, was also given the privilege of the position.

Caiaphas is revealed in the New Testament as being unscrupulous, a master of intrigue and conspiracy. Thus he is the one to tell the others that it is expedient that one man should die that the nation not perish. He initiates the murder plot that will lead to the crucifixion. And yet his words were unintentionally prophetic.

Caiaphas was of the House of Annas. Interestingly, the rabbis in the Talmud have this to say of the House of Annas: "Woe to the family of Annas! Woe to the serpentlike hisses" (Pes 57a).[1] The implication is of the serpent-like sounds, whispers, of plots, deception, and conspiracy.

King Solomon: The dedicator

Hebrew: *Shlomo*, meaning "peaceful"

King Solomon appears in *The Harbinger* as the king who oversaw the dedication on the Temple Mount. The son of King David, Solomon reigned over the united kingdom of Israel at the height of its power and prosperity and in an era of unprecedented peace. He was famed for both his wisdom and affluence. It was Solomon who built the Temple of Jerusalem. Solomon began his reign not only with great wisdom but also with great devotion to God and His ways. But as time went on, his heart began to turn away from this devotion and to other gods. Solomon's apostasy resulted in the united kingdom of Israel being divided in the northern kingdom (Israel) and the southern kingdom (Judah). Solomon is regarded as the traditional author of the Book of Proverbs, Ecclesiastes, and the Song of Solomon.

Jesus: The Messiah

Hebrew: *Yeshua*, meaning "God is salvation"

The central figure of *The Harbinger* is ultimately Yeshua (Jesus) as the book leads up to the chapter entitled "Eternity." *The Harbinger* presents the issue of judgment. But that issue ultimately leads up to the answer. The answer is presented in the name *Yeshua* or, in English, *Jesus*.

Yeshua/Jesus is the center of the New Testament. Taking into account the prophecies of Messiah, He is the center of Scripture itself. He remains the center of human history. The calendar divides around His birth, every year of every date being identified by the distance in which it stands from the nativity.

Twenty centuries after His birth, He remains the center of controversy, the center of debate. Time has not diminished His influence. He remains the most influential, history-changing, world-changing, and life-changing person in human history.

The same One who happens to be the central figure of human history also happens to be the One who fulfills the words of the Hebrew prophets concerning the Messiah.

That He has become all this—not by power, not by riches, not by position, and not by the sword, but by a life of love culminating with

His death on a crucifixion stake—is something that defies all the laws of the very history of which He is the center.

He asked His disciples, "Who do you say I am?" That remains the issue. His name means "'Salvation." But whether He is our salvation depends on how we answer that ultimate question.

Chapter 15

EXPLORING *the* BIBLICAL WORLD

Uncovering The Harbinger's *Ancient Backdrop*

T HE POWER THAT carried out the invasion of Israel, the backdrop of Isaiah 9:10 and the harbingers, and that would end up causing Israel's destruction was the Assyrian Empire.

The Assyrian kingdom was centered on the Tigris River in northern Mesopotamia (now Iraq) and named after its first capital city, Ashur. Beginning in the tenth century BC, Assyria began its ascension to world power, conquering the kingdoms of Egypt, Babylonia, Syria, Phoenicia, and Persia, to name a few. For three centuries the Assyrians controlled the entire Fertile Crescent, from Egypt to the Persian Gulf.

The Assyrians are credited with inventing the 24-hour day, the 60-minute hour, the 60-second minute, the 360-degree circle, the 360-day year divided up into 12 months, and making great strides in the study of astronomy.

At the same time they were among the most cruel and feared people ever to walk the sands of the Middle East. The Assyrian state was largely devoted to maintaining its military power and dominance over Mesopotamia. They invented such siege machines as the battering ram and mobile towers.

The Assyrians are famous for one other contribution to world history—terrorism—defined as the strategic use of terror to accomplish a political aim. Under the Assyrians entire populations of besieged towns would be massacred. Skin would be nailed to city walls, outside of which would stand mountains of human heads. The Assyrians would mutilate their victims and put them on display so that none would be foolish enough to rise up against their rule. So effective was Assyrian terror that entire cities and regions would surrender to their armies without a fight.

So the shadow or threat of Assyria, which loomed in the background of the Israel of Isaiah's day, was especially menacing. The prospect of having the Assyrian army come to one's walls, as happened to the city of Samaria, was almost unbearably fearful.

In 722 BC the Assyrian Empire wiped the northern kingdom of Israel off the face of the map. But the prophets of Israel foretold the Assyrian Empire's ultimate destruction. Their end would come in 612 BC after the Medes to the east and the Babylonians from the south would rise up against them and, likewise, wipe their kingdom off the face of the earth, so thoroughly that passersby would be hard pressed to identify the empire that once thrived in the site that was now nothing but ruins.

The Northern Kingdom of Israel: The Nation Under Judgment

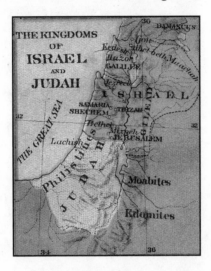

Israel, also known as the northern kingdom and Samaria, is the backdrop of Isaiah 9:10. It was to this kingdom that the Nine Harbingers appear. It was this kingdom that defied God's warnings in 732 BC, and this kingdom that, in 722 BC was wiped off the face of the earth.

The northern kingdom of Israel was formed out of the division of the united kingdom under Solomon. Upon Solomon's death in the tenth century BC, the ten tribes to the north refused to accept the reign of Solomon's son Rehoboam. Instead they followed the usurper Jeroboam, who founded the northern kingdom. Later on, Samaria was made the capital city. The people of the northern kingdom vacillated between the worship of God and the worship of the Phoenician Baal. Under the reign of such rulers as Ahab and Jezebel, those who were faithful to God were persecuted, including the prophet Elijah.

The Kingdom's End in 722 BC

Over time the northern kingdom fell further and further away from God and His ways, increasingly resembling the pagan nations that surrounded it. As the nation continued its spiritual and cultural decline, the power and influence of the Assyrian Kingdom continued to rise. The Israelite king Pekah decided to make a stand against Assyrian domination and called on the southern kingdom to join him. When King Ahaz of Judah refused, Pekah attacked Jerusalem. Ahaz sent word to Tiglath Pileser III, king of Assyria, to help him. With that, Assyria invaded the northern kingdom. This is the invasion on the land in 732 BC that sets the ancient backdrop of *The Harbinger*. It was in response to this calamity that the people and leaders of Israel uttered the defiant vow of Isaiah 9:10. They vowed to rise up stronger than before. It was this spirit that would ultimately lead to the nation's destruction.

King Pekah was deposed. Though his replacement, Hoshea, began his reign in submission to Assyria, soon he grew confident enough to attempt a rebellion. Around the year 727 BC he ceased the annual payment of tribute to the Assyrian king and sent messengers to Egypt to form an anti-Assyrian alliance. In 724 BC the new king of Assyria, Shalmaneser V, marched into the northern kingdom and threw King Hoshea in chains. Shalmaneser laid siege to Israel's capital city of Samaria but was forced to return to Nineveh. Sargon, his younger brother, was left in command of the army. Two years later Shalmaneser died. Sargon, now king, pressed the siege. In 722 BC the city of Samaria fell to the invaders. The city was burned to the ground, and the survivors were removed from the land.

This is the destruction of which the prophet Isaiah prophesied in the verses that followed Isaiah 9:10.

The northern kingdom would never rise again. Most of its inhabitants would disappear among the nations, known from then on as "The Ten Lost Tribes of Israel."

Chapter 16

WHO IS *"the* PROPHET"?

(Special Feature From FrontLine)

WHO IS THE prophet? This is one of the most often asked questions. Some have suggested that the prophet is the author, Jonathan Cahn. Others have speculated that the prophet was a mysterious stranger who revealed these things to Jonathan and asked him to write the book.

What's the answer?

First, what is a prophet? The Hebrew word for prophet is *navi*. The word refers to one who speaks by inspiration from God. The Greek word *prophetace* refers to one who foretells the future or who simply forth tells what God is saying by inspiration from God. Prophets appear throughout the Hebrew Scriptures. In the New Covenant Scriptures, several people are spoken of as prophets or as those who prophesy, including Simeon, Anna, Yochanan (John the Baptist), Agabus, and so forth, and, of course, the Messiah Himself.

The Harbinger does not get into the doctrinal issue of the place, existence, or role of prophets today. Though people have called Jonathan Cahn a prophet, he would only refer to himself as a watchman.

Then who is the prophet? Since *The Harbinger* involves the warning, the alarm, the revelations, and calling of the Hebrew prophets as they spoke to the nation of Israel, the prophet is a representative of the prophetic voice or Hebrew Scripture, a modern embodiment and translation of the Hebrew prophets.

Thus, in *The Harbinger*, Nouriel describes the prophet's appearance this way:

> "What did he look like?"
> "Somewhat thin, dark hair, a closely cropped beard. He was Mediterranean or Middle Eastern looking."[1]

The Hebrew prophets would be bearded and of Mediterranean or Middle Eastern appearance. And like many of the prophets of Israel, his origins and his end are not known. So Nouriel has no idea from where he comes or where he goes.

> "And when will we meet again?" I asked.
> "When it's time to speak of the First Harbinger."
> "Here?"
> "At the appointed place," he replied.
> "How will I know?"
> "How did you know to come here in the first place?" he asked.
> "I didn't."
> "So you won't know again, and yet you'll be there."
> And then he was gone.[2]

He is a composite. In some ways he is representative of the prophet Isaiah, as it is Isaiah's prophecy that underlies *The Harbinger*. In other ways he parallels the prophet Jeremiah, as he carries a burden to warn his own nation in the face of apostasy and coming judgment as well as what he reveals to Nouriel near the ending:

> "'And Jeremiah commanded Baruch, saying, "I am confined, I cannot go into the house of the LORD. You go, therefore, and read from the scroll which you have written at my instruction, the words of the LORD, in the hearing of the people in the LORD's house on the day of fasting. And you shall also read them in the hearing of all Judah who come from their cities."'[3]
>
> "Jeremiah's movements were restricted. He couldn't deliver his prophecy in public, not in person. So he sent Baruch in his place so that the prophecy would be proclaimed publicly to all. So Baruch wasn't only Jeremiah's scribe but also, at times, his representative, his voice."
>
> "Why are you telling me this?"
>
> "Because I too am restricted. So you must go and make known the message, to give them the warning and the hope."[4]

The connection to the prophet Jeremiah becomes crucial to the mystery of the final seal and the calling of Nouriel. But the prophet is a composite not only of Jeremiah and Isaiah but also of all the prophets who ever brought forth a word to a nation.

Though in the narrative the prophet appears to know what he couldn't have known by natural ability, for example, where and when their next encounters will be, what he actually reveals to Nouriel is not based on any spiritual or supernatural gift of his own but rather on the prophetic revelation of Scripture concerning national judgment. Thus the prophet relays to Nouriel the biblical template, pattern, and signs of a nation in danger of judgment, all of which are now reappearing to America.

Of course, it is Jonathan Cahn speaking through the prophet, just as he speaks through all the characters in *The Harbinger*. Through the prophet the revelations of *The Harbinger* that Jonathan first shared to his congregation are imparted not only to Nouriel but also to the reader. In other words, the prophet is a vessel, a narrative instrument, a prophetic figure to appropriately represent and bring forth a prophetic mystery and warning.

Though the prophet is a literary figure to bring forth the message of *The Harbinger,* he does have a connection in reality—only it wasn't that he was based on a specific person but rather that he foreshadowed one.

After Jonathan finished writing the book, the scene in which the prophet first appeared was re-created in real life. (See chapter 24, "The Story Behind the Story.") When Nouriel first encountered the prophet, he sat down in a public place. Next to him, to his left, was a stranger, the man he would call "the prophet." The week that Jonathan finished writing *The Harbinger* and had to decide what to do with it, how to proceed, he was at the airport at Charlotte, North Carolina, in between flights. He sat down in a public place, and next to him sat a stranger to his left.

In the book Nouriel is pondering a small object he holds in his hands, a seal. Jonathan was holding a small object he was holding in his hands, a pocket Bible. In the book the stranger turns to Nouriel and initiates a conversation, with small talk, concerning the object in his hands, the seal. At the airport the stranger turns to Jonathan and initiates a conversation, with small talk, concerning the object in his hands, the Bible.

In the book the prophet suddenly begins to speak prophetically to Nouriel. The man in the airport suddenly begins to speak prophetically to Jonathan. The words of the prophet to Nouriel will ultimately lead him to write a book that brings a prophetic warning to America. The words of the stranger in the airport will cause *The Harbinger* to become a book through which a prophetic warning will go forth to America.

So though the prophet in *The Harbinger* is a fictional figure serving as a vessel and instrument to bring forth the message of *The Harbinger*—it turns out that the figure of the prophet was itself prophetic of one who would be a vessel to bring forth *The Harbinger*—for real.

Chapter 17

WHO IS NOURIEL?

(Special Feature From FrontLine)

W HO IS NOURIEL? This is another of the most often asked questions. Some have suggested that Nouriel is Jonathan Cahn. The evidence? Nouriel is an author. Jonathan is an author. Nouriel is Jewish, a descendant of Aaron. Jonathan is Jewish and a descendant of Aaron. Nouriel brings forth a prophetic warning to America involving the words of a prophet. Jonathan writes *The Harbinger*, which brings forth a prophetic word involving the words of a prophet. But is this the answer?

Jonathan did write *The Harbinger*, but he didn't receive the revelations from any other person or figure. As the author, Jonathan is, of course, speaking through the words of Nouriel just as he is speaking through the words of the prophet.

It could be noted that his full name Baruch Nouriel connects with the names of two famous figures on the scene at the time of *The Harbinger* being written, both linked to America in the wake of the economic collapse. "Baruch" is similar to "Barack." Growing up, Baruch calls himself "Barry." Barack Obama did the same. Other than *The Harbinger*, the name *Nouriel* is most famous for being that of an economist, Nouriel Roubini. Nicknamed "Dr. Doom," Roubini is known for predicting, through economic analysis, the collapse of the American and global economy in 2008.[1] All of these themes have parallels in *The Harbinger*. But the connection here was not intentional.

Then who is Nouriel?

As the prophet is a narrative vessel and instrument for the giving of the revelation of *The Harbinger*, Nouriel is the narrative vessel and instrument for its *receiving*. He asks questions that the reader or hearer would ask. He reacts as would react the reader or the hearer.

The last mystery of *The Harbinger* is the mystery of Nouriel himself. As with the other mysteries, the prophet reveals it:

> "Your name," he said, "is Baruch Nouriel. The name of Jeremiah's scribe was *Baruch ben Neriah*—*Neriah* meaning, *the light of God* or *the flame of God*. Do you know what *Nouriel* means?"
> "No."
> "Nouriel means *the flame of God*. In effect, it's the same name."
> "What are you saying?" I asked, my voice now shaking.
> "*You*, Nouriel…you are the final mystery. You're the mystery looking in the mirror and not recognizing that the image is you."[2]

The prophet reveals that Nouriel's first name is not *Nouriel* but *Baruch*. *Baruch*, the opening word for most Hebrew prayers, means "blessed." More to the point, *Baruch* is the name of a biblical figure, the scribe of the prophet Jeremiah. The scribes, or the *sofrim*, were those appointed to write down the Word of God on sheets of parchment. They were the preservers of Scripture. The word could refer to those who simply reproduced the words of other scrolls, passing Scripture from generation to generation. The word could also refer to those who first committed the Word of God to written form at the dictation of a prophet. Baruch was of the latter category. He personally recorded the words of Jeremiah that they could go forth to the nation and be preserved for future generations. The prophet links Nouriel to Baruch in that Nouriel is called to write down the prophetic message in the form of a book that it might go forth to the nation.

Baruch was Jewish.

So is Nouriel.

Baruch is traditionally viewed as being of the priestly line.

So is Nouriel.

Baruch is a *sofer,* one who writes.

So too Nouriel, by profession, is a writer.

Baruch was called to record the words of Jeremiah.

Nouriel is told by the prophet to always keep on hand a recording device at every encounter that the prophet's words would be recorded.

An interesting footnote—just as the figure of the prophet turned out to be prophetic of a real person, at least in one instance, so too is the figure of Nouriel. A few months after *The Harbinger* was released, a man appeared at the Jerusalem Center to introduce himself to Jonathan. In the book Nouriel's first and last name is Baruch Kaplan, though he chose for years to be known as Barry Kaplan. The man who came to see Jonathan was Baruch Kaplan, but he had often gone by Barry Kaplan.

Like Baruch Kaplan (Nouriel) in the book, the man was Jewish. Like Nouriel, he was a believer in Yeshua, Jesus, as the Jewish Messiah. As with Nouriel, he lived in New York City. As with Nouriel, he was connected with Wall Street and the area of St. Paul's Chapel. As with Nouriel, he was connected with 9/11, being there on the day of the calamity. And as with Nouriel, he was devoting his life to getting the message out of salvation. He had picked up a copy of *The Harbinger,* and when he turned to the last pages, where the prophet reveals the mystery of Nouriel, he was blown away and had to meet the man who wrote the book.

In short, Nouriel is another vessel by which the message is to go forth. As the prophet parallels Jeremiah, so Nouriel parallels Baruch.

But as the prophet is a representation of more than one prophet but a composite of all the prophets, all those who gave the prophetic word, so Nouriel is a representation and composite not just of one scribe, but of all those who have received, recorded, and transmitted the Word of God that it might go forth to those who needed to hear it.

Chapter 18

The SEALS
(and the SEAL BEHIND the SEALS)

I n *THE HARBINGER* the mysteries are revealed through the giving of nine seals. What is a seal? The word for seal in the Hebrew Scriptures is *chotam*. It comes from a root verb that means to mark, to seal, make an end, close up. The ancient seal was a stamp or an engraving made out of some hard substance such as stone, metal, or crystal. It would be impressed upon a softer substance such as a clay or wax, also known as a seal.

The resulting seal would most often be affixed to a document. The seal denoted authority, power, and irreversibility. In the Book of Esther the king's seal is used to issue an order to save the Jews:

> You yourselves write a decree concerning the Jews, as you please, in the king's name, and seal it with the king's signet ring: for whatever is written in the king's name and sealed with the king's signet ring no one can revoke.
>
> —ESTHER 8:8

The Sign of Prophecy

So the seal would become a symbol for a word or decree originating from God. In the Book of Daniel, the ninth chapter, the prophet is given a prophecy containing a mathematical countdown until the coming of the Messiah. In this word, he is told that the time period was given "*to seal up vision and prophecy*" (v. 24). A prophetic word from God was as a document of authority or a decree from a king.

A seal would also bear witness to the identity and ownership of the one behind it. The seal would also guarantee the document's security. The sealed document or book could not be opened except by the one to whom it was intended, the one given the authority to open it. Again, one can see the connection to a prophetic word from God. So in Isaiah 29:11, this word is given concerning prophecy:

> The whole vision has become to you like the words of a book that is sealed, which men deliver to one who is literate, saying, "Read this, please." And he says, "I cannot, for it is sealed."

So a prophetic message can be likened to a document with a seal on it, one that may be hidden for a time and only opened and read at the time appointed. So the prophet Daniel is given this instruction:

> But you, Daniel, shut up the words, and seal the book until the time of the end; many shall run to and fro, and knowledge shall increase.
>
> —DANIEL 12:4

The Book of Revelation is, by definition, a book of revealing. So it is no accident that within the book much of the prophetic revelations given come through the image of seals being opened.

The Nine Seals

This is the background of the nine seals that appear in *The Harbinger*. The seals denote that Nouriel is going to be given a message of importance, a prophetic word for a nation. Just as seals on a document had to be opened, so Nouriel must "open" each seal by deciphering the mystery it holds. He must "break open" the following seals:

- **The Seal of the First Harbinger**—a simple line that descends and ascends in a V-like formation—Symbol of the Breach
- **The Seal of the Second Harbinger**—a more complex image of ancient peoples as if taken from a bas relief—Symbol of the Terrorist
- **The Seal of the Third Harbinger**—a conglomerate of shapes with no particular order—Symbol of the Bricks

- **The Seal of the Fourth Harbinger**—an image of a ziggurat—Symbol of the Tower

- **The Seal of the Fifth Harbinger**—an irregular line that is taken to represent the top of a mountain—Symbol of the Gazit Stone

- **The Seal of the Sixth Harbinger**—an image of a tree—Symbol of the Sycamore

- **The Seal of the Seventh Harbinger**—an image of a different tree—Symbol of the Erez Tree

- **The Seal of the Eighth Harbinger**—an image of a platform—Symbol of the Utterance

- **The Seal of the Ninth Harbinger**—an image of a parchment—Symbol of the Prophecy

In addition, some of the seals contain more than one image and are revealed to hold still other and deeper meanings.

So as much as a seal represents a message sent forth, each of the nine seals comprise a message sent forth. As much as a seal may represent a prophetic word, so that is the nature of what Nouriel is being given. As much as a seal represents a closing, or shut up message, so until he can decipher it, the word or mystery is closed. And as much as a seal may be broken open, so that is Nouriel's mission, to break open each seal that its mystery and message may be revealed.

The Mystery of the Last Seal

But there is more than nine seals in *The Harbinger*. There is one more, the seal that comes before the nine but sets the stage and then that reappears at the end to *seal* everything up. What was on the last seal? Nouriel describes it to Ana:

> "The writing on the seal was in a language I had never seen before. But I remembered the words of the prophet that day we first met on the bench, when he took the seal to examine it. He said it was Hebrew, but a different form of Hebrew—Paleo-Hebrew, an older version."[1]

The last seal is different from the rest in that it consists solely of letters in Paleo-Hebrew, an ancient form of Hebrew prevalent in the time before the Babylonian Captivity. The words read:

"Baruchyahu Ben Neriyahu Ha Sofer."[2]

The words are revealed to signify the identity of Baruch, the scribe of the prophet Jeremiah. But what most readers of *The Harbinger* will not realize when they read this is that this first and last seal *actually exists.* In fact, it was the existence of this seal that inspired the rest.

Image by Maurice Thompson/
© Geoff Tucker of Visual Bible Journeys

It was discovered in 1975 in the shop of an antiquities dealer in Jerusalem. From the style of the letters, scholars dated the seal to the sixth century BC, the time period in which Jeremiah prophesied. The words are arranged in three lines. They read, "Berechyahu, son of Neriyahu, the scribe."[3] The words match exactly what is written of Baruch, the scribe of Jeremiah, in the Bible. And as a scribe, it is virtually certain that he would have had a seal. The object is known as

"Baruch's Seal." In the spring of 1996 the discovery of another ancient seal bearing the same imprint was made. Both seals also bear a fingerprint. It is speculated that this could be the very fingerprint of the biblical figure.

In *The Harbinger* it was the Seal of Baruch that leads Nouriel on a journey of nine seals, a journey that will end with his writing a book. And in reality, it was the real Seal of Baruch that led Jonathan Cahn to write of the nine seals and the book known as *The Harbinger*.

Chapter 19

FREQUENTLY ASKED QUESTIONS ABOUT
The HARBINGER and JONATHAN CAHN

(Plus Some Key Confusions Out There;
Special Feature From FrontLine)

Why did Jonathan Cahn decide to write *The Harbinger* in the form of a narrative?

He originally wrote it as nonfiction. *The Harbinger* contains many deep connections, and his goal was to reach as many people as possible. In the Bible, spiritual truths are often communicated through narrative, parables, symbolism, pictures, images, and allegory. So the truths and revelations of *The Harbinger* were put into this form in order to reach as many people as possible.

How do you tell which part of *The Harbinger* is true?

The majority is real. The revelation is real, but the narrative surrounding or framing the revelation is fiction—the prophet, Nouriel, Ana, their encounters, the seals, the dream, etc. But that which is revealed through the prophet, that which he shows to Nouriel, the ancient mystery, the biblical template of judgment, the signs, current events, and reappearing of the harbingers in America—all that is revealed, is real.

People have called Jonathan Cahn a prophet. Does he claim to be a prophet?

No. Jonathan Cahn never calls himself a prophet. He would call himself a watchman.

How did Jonathan Cahn get these revelations?

He was led. Soon after 9/11 he was in prayer and was led to the section of Scripture that speaks of Israel's opening act of judgment, the

171

strike of the Assyrians. It was the same section in which is contained the key scripture of *The Harbinger*, Isaiah 9:10.

Did anyone else *get* the connections or receive any revelation like this?

There is no way to know whether God has revealed these same truths to anyone else or not. One similar message that Jonathan is aware of happened soon after 9/11. Pastor David Wilkerson, author of *The Cross and the Switchblade* and founder of Teen Challenge, spoke to his church in New York City as to what he believed God's message was to America in the wake of 9/11. He then spoke of the same ancient events, the same section of Scripture, and even quoted the same verse, Isaiah 9:10. He didn't do any of this because he was aware of the harbingers, as most had either not yet happened or not become known.

Has *The Harbinger* been accepted or endorsed by any prominent religious figures, Bible teachers, pastors, or leaders?

Yes. *The Harbinger* has been enthusiastically endorsed by key leaders from Pat Boone to Pat Robertson, Bible and seminary professors, and ministers from a broad spectrum: Baptist to charismatic as well as other denominations. Across the nation, congregations and Bible studies are teaching, sharing, and spreading its message, along with individual readers, religious and secular.

What are Jonathan Cahn's spiritual beliefs?

Jonathan Cahn believes the Bible is the Word of God. He is a Jewish believer in Jesus (Yeshua) as the Messiah promised to the Jewish people and then to the world. He is the leader of the Jerusalem Center/Beth Israel in Wayne, New Jersey, where he has taught the Word of God for years. He is also president of Hope of the World ministries, an outreach of the Word and projects of compassion to the needy. He has in the past been asked by the Billy Graham Evangelistic Association to provide special counseling at various events.

Do words like *mystery*, *secret*, or *hidden* have anything to do with mysticism?

No. The Bible itself uses all of these words. In the case of *The Harbinger*, it simply refers to the fact that something is being revealed.

Is *The Harbinger* written for believers or nonbelievers?

Both. *The Harbinger* is written in such a way as to call the believer to repentance and revival and the nonbeliever to salvation.

Can what happened in ancient Israel be applied to America?

In Romans 15:4 it is written that "everything that was written in the past was written to teach us" (NIV). If that which took place in ancient Israel were not applicable to us today, most preaching would have to cease.

Is such a revelation beyond the Bible's parameters?

The Bible reveals that God is righteous, He judges sin and nations, He sends warning, and He acts in a manner consistent with His Word. *The Harbinger* is simply revealing that this is happening in reality—that the biblical template of judgment in Isaiah is replaying now before our eyes. This is all solidly within sound scriptural parameters.

Does *The Harbinger* say that God has made a covenant with America and that America has somehow replaced Israel, or does it advocate some form of Replacement Theology?

No. *The Harbinger* notes that American civilization was founded by the Puritans, who envisioned it after the pattern of ancient Israel, who dedicated it to God, and who believed that they were in covenant with God. This is all historical fact. The question of whether God has honored their dedication is left open. But the historical fact is noted only as it forms a striking background to the fact that America has followed the same pattern of ancient Israel's apostasy and is now witnessing the same pattern of judgment. But none of the mysteries revealed in *The Harbinger* are dependent on this background. And none of this has any bearing on Israel's calling as God's covenant nation.

Does *The Harbinger* say that Isaiah was prophesying of America?

No. This comes from a fundamental misunderstanding. *The Harbinger* never says that Isaiah was prophesying of America—but of ancient Israel. What it does say is that the biblical template and warnings of national judgment that manifested in the last days of ancient Israel are now manifesting and replaying in America, precisely, eerily, and uncannily.

What does this have to do with hermeneutics?

Very little. Hermeneutics concerns the interpretation of a given text. *The Harbinger* fully affirms that the text of Isaiah's prophecy is about ancient Israel—thus no hermeneutical issue exists. The use of the biblical template in Isaiah to give warning in no way alters or even touches the original meaning, context, or interpretation (hermeneutics) of Scripture.

There have been some extreme ideas hurled in the direction of *The Harbinger*—everything from Replacement Theology to Freemasonry, etc. Is there any connection?

Not in any way. When anything becomes as large as *The Harbinger* has become, it invites all sorts of confusion and misperception. The bizarre and confused nature of such disparate and contradictory notions only shows the impact *The Harbinger* is making. One observer thus noted: "The strangeness of the attacks against *The Harbinger* have to make you wonder what the devil has against it."[1]

Does *The Harbinger* say that God was on the side of the terrorists?

Not at all, no more so than the Bible says that God was on the side of the ancient Assyrians when He allowed them to attack His land. God was against such evil then as well as now. God is against all evil, but He will use all things, good and evil, for good, for redemption.

Are the modern harbingers literal fulfillments of Isaiah's prophecy?

No. They are biblical *signs,* manifestations, and warnings in a biblical pattern or template of judgment. Because some have confused that issue, they've mistakenly argued over the differences in the modern manifestations as opposed to the ancient. If one were to go by such logic, one could only accept the harbingers if New York City were invaded by spear-throwing Assyrians attacking buildings made of clay bricks and if Americans responded in perfect ancient Hebrew dialects.

Does *The Harbinger* say that victims of such national calamities as 9/11 were under judgment?

No, no more so than Abraham Lincoln, when he spoke of the Civil War as a national judgment of America, was saying that those wounded or killed were being individually judged—and no more than the Bible says such things when it speaks of the national judgment of Israel. *The Harbinger* very clearly distinguishes the differences between the realm of individual experience and that of national judgment.

Isaiah is from the Old Testament. How can we say that God can act in a similar way in the New Testament age?

First, it's never wise to tell God what He can and cannot do. Second, God is the same yesterday, today, and forever. There is nothing in the New Testament that says God no longer brings judgment against sin or nations. In fact, it says the very opposite.

If God is good, and a God of love, how can He bring judgment?

It's the other way around. If God did not judge what is evil, He could not be good. Love must oppose what is evil. And yet the message of the Bible is that this same love would put itself in the place of those being judged if it would result in their being saved.

How are signs different from fulfillments?

The point of the harbingers, or warning signs, is to give warning, to speak. The modern signs *correspond* to the ancient signs but *speak* to a modern nation just as the ancient harbingers once did to an ancient one. For example, the sign of the sycamore in ancient Israel was a Middle Eastern sycamore appearing to a Middle Eastern nation, but the sign of the sycamore in America was a Western version of the sycamore appearing to a Western nation. On the other hand, some have attempted to argue that the Seventh Harbinger technically belongs to the spruce family and not the cedar as in Isaiah. But neither Isaiah nor the ancient Israelites spoke English or used the word *cedar*. They used the Hebrew word *erez*, which, actually and most exactly, refers to a pinacea tree, which includes both what we would today call a cedar and the spruce, among others. And it was an erez tree that manifested at the corner of Ground Zero.

Is it possible that one can make statistics say anything we want?

Statistics can be used in a biased way (as in politics, ideology, etc.), but no amount of statistic handling could produce anything remotely like what is presented in *The Harbinger*. For example, the chapter entitled "The Mystery of the Shemitah" reveals the two greatest crashes in American history up to September of 2008. Each took place on the *same exact biblical day*, a day that comes around once in seven years; each occurred exactly seven biblical years from the other, on the day appointed in *Scripture to wipe away the financial accounts* of a nation. Nothing could have constructed that except for the absolute reality of the fact.

Why does an argument of coincidence not hold up with regard to the harbingers?

The problem is coincidences are not consistent—but the harbingers are. Every one of the Nine Harbingers of Israel's judgment and, specifically, of Isaiah 9:10, have, in one form or another, appeared in America. Each of these is joined together in the specific biblical template and verse. Each of them is linked to 9/11. Most became *actual symbols* of 9/11. No one person or organization was behind making all nine of these harbingers manifest as they did.

For example, an American leader proclaimed the ancient (and obscure) vow of judgment in Isaiah 9:10, word for word, on the very day after 9/11—from Capitol Hill. He mentioned a stone that would go up on the ground of destruction, where the bricks had fallen. He could have no possible idea that three years later this very thing would happen. He spoke of a tree being struck down by the calamity and being replaced by another. He could have no idea that on the very day he said that, the tree was being discovered, and three years later, the act of replacement would take place in the form of a ceremony. The truth is the manifestation of all nine harbingers in a consistent progression has never happened before in American history, or world history, except one other time—in the last days of ancient Israel, before its judgment. One analyst did a statistical analysis of just two of the many connections in *The Harbinger* and found the odds to be astronomically against coincidence.[2]

Have there been any secular or government leaders who have read *The Harbinger* and taken its message to heart?

Yes. *The Harbinger* has been read by government leaders, members of legislatures in various states across the country, and on Capitol Hill by senators and members of Congress, who have indeed taken the message to heart.

Is *The Harbinger* political?

No. It's not about politics; it's about God. Though the issues raised by *The Harbinger* touch every realm of life, they transcend politics. There is no agenda except to sound the warning and call those who will hear to salvation and the will of God.

Does *The Harbinger* give hope?

Absolutely. If there was no hope, there would be no harbingers and no book called *The Harbinger*. One gives warning when there's hope of heeding it. *The Harbinger* presents not only the problem and the warning but also the answer and the hope. An entire chapter is devoted to presenting hope for the individual and another for a people and a nation.

How long did it take Jonathan Cahn to write *The Harbinger*?

Once he began writing it in the narrative form in which it appears today, it happened rapidly. It took about four months, and that with his being able to work on it only in his spare time, a few hours a few times a week. Every time he sat down, the words would stream into the computer as if the words had already existed before he typed them.

Does *The Harbinger* lift up Jesus as the answer?

Absolutely. His real name, *Yeshua,* literally means salvation. First comes the reality and warning of judgment, and then the answer of salvation.

Chapter 20

SIGNS *of the* END

What Bible Prophecy Says of the Last Days

BIBLICAL PROPHECY SPEAKS of what is called "the last days," "the end of the age," and "the end of days." In the New Testament this is revealed as the time before the second coming of the Messiah and the kingdom of God on earth. End-time prophecy presents both an overall or general picture of the end times as well as providing specific detail.

Here are a few of the things foretold of the last days in biblical prophecy:

Prophecy	Status
There will be a great "apostasy" or "falling away" from faith.	Happening
There will be a great move toward immorality.	Happening
Men will be "lovers of selves."	Happening
An age of covetousness	Happening
An age of blasphemy	Moving in that direction
An age of arrogance	Happening
An age of man without natural affection	Moving in that direction
An age that despises those who are good	Moving in that direction
An age of pleasure seeking	Happening
Knowledge shall increase.	Happening
Travel shall increase.	Happening
Globalization: the emergence of a one-world civilization	Happening
Unification: the emergence of a one-world government	Moving in that direction
Persecution of believers	Happening in some places and moving in that direction in others
Natural disasters	Happening
The gospel of salvation shall be proclaimed to all nations.	Happening
The Jewish people shall return from the nations to their ancient homeland.	Happening
Israel shall again become a nation.	Happened: 1948
Jerusalem shall again belong to Israel and the Jewish people.	Happened: 1967

Prophecy	Status
The Jewish people shall again fight in the land of Israel.	Happened
The land of Israel will blossom as a rose in the desert.	Happened
The world will center on the Middle East.	Happening
The world will center on the issue of Jerusalem.	Happening
Jerusalem will be the center of controversy.	Happening
There will be in some way a reviving of the Roman Empire in modern form.	Not yet
One man will rule the world—the Antichrist.	Not yet
The Temple of Jerusalem will be rebuilt.	Not yet
All the world will come against Israel.	Not yet militarily, but the world is aligning against Israel.
There will be a great power in the Orient able to marshal a massive army.	Exists
The entire world will be able to view a single event at the same time.	Already is
Man will have the power to control every financial transaction in the world.	Moving in that direction
The Jewish people will begin to return to their Messiah, Yeshua, Jesus.	Happening

Chapter 21

WHERE IS AMERICA
in END-TIME PROPHECY?

And What This Has to Do With The Harbinger

THE QUESTION IS inevitably asked, "Where is America in the Bible? Where does it appear in end-time prophecy?"

Since the Bible does speak of specific events and nations in end-time prophecy, shouldn't we expect to see America mentioned? After all, America has been the preeminent world power of modern times.

Some have come up with answers.

Tarshish and All Her Villages

In Ezekiel 38:13 it is written:

> Sheba, Dedan, the merchants of Tarshish, and all their young lions...

The claim is that the *Tarshish* mentioned here is Great Britain, and thus "all their young lions" (also translated as "villages") is a reference to all her former colonies, which would include the United States. Either way the problem here is that there is no certain way of identifying Tarshish with Great Britain. And even if there were, the identification would be little more than a minor and general mention.

The Isles and Coastlands

Ezekiel 39:6 says this:

> And I will send fire on Magog and on those who live in security in the coastlands. Then they shall know that I am the LORD.

The argument here is that the word for "coastlands" or "isles" refers to far-off lands that could be overseas. America is certainly a far-off land from Israel and overseas. And the Scripture certainly could include America in the event of which it speaks. But the problem is that the word here is so inclusive and general that there is no way that we could derive from this a clear identification or role for America in end-time prophecy.

Babylon

Others have identified America with the Babylon spoken of in the Book of Revelation:

> After these things I saw another angel coming down from heaven, having great authority, and the earth was illuminated with his glory. And he cried mightily with a loud voice, saying, "Babylon the great is fallen, is fallen, and has become a dwelling place of demons, a prison for every foul spirit, and a cage for every unclean and hated bird! For all the nations have drunk of the wine of the wrath of her fornication, the kings of the earth have committed fornication with her, and the merchants of the earth have become rich through the abundance of her luxury."
>
> —REVELATION 18:1–3

The argument is that the Babylon of Revelation is a predominant world power. It is a power of great wealth and opulence. It trades with the world. It affects the entire world. It corrupts the world with immorality.

The problem with this identification, among other things, is that much the same thing could be said of other nations, kingdoms, or empires at the height of their power and prosperity. The interpretation is built upon the presumption that America will hold the same global preeminence at the end of the age that it does now. The argument becomes circular. Further, it speaks of Babylon as a city. Beyond that, it speaks of a connection to seven hills, which is historically the identity given to Rome. Others believe it will be the literal city of Babylon.

One can speak of the "spirit of Babylon" in various world powers, including that of America. But to say that the Babylon of Revelation *is* America requires a high degree of stretching.

The Eagle

Still others believe that passages in the Bible that speak of eagles in symbolic contexts refer to America. Such interpretations are based on the fact that the eagle is a universally accepted symbol of America.

The problem here is that the eagle is many things and has been used as a symbol of many things for ages. In fact, the eagle has been a symbol of many other nations or empires, most notably that of Rome. Without more evidence and context to point to America, we have no more reason to identify the eagle with America than any other nation represented by this symbol or, for that matter, any other power or attribute.

The Missing Superpower

So what is the conclusion?

Whether we like it or not, while other nations are clearly mentioned in biblical prophecy, America is not one of them. There is no clear reference to America in end-time prophecy that would identify it as a major power. What does this mean?

There is a saying that the absence of evidence is not evidence of absence. But in the case of America and end-time prophecy, the absence of evidence *is* evidence of absence—at least as much as it concerns a superpower. If America were to maintain its position as the leading, reigning, or preeminent superpower at the very end of the age, it would have to be mentioned in end-time prophecy. That it is not mentioned is evidence that it will no longer be the world's preeminent superpower that it presently is.

What This Has to Do With *The Harbinger*

What does this have to do with *The Harbinger*? Everything. The absence of America in biblical prophecy points to a world where America no longer leads, is no longer the head of nations. How do we go from where we are now to that end-time scenario? What is presented in *The Harbinger* would fill in that gap.

What it points to is this: If America does not turn back to God, then the blessings it has long known will be removed. Those blessings include its prosperity, its peace, its world power, and its global preeminence. In fact, if America continues on its present course, one of the first things we can expect is the removal of the crown it has worn for most of the twentieth century—that of "head of nations." According to the ancient mystery and pattern in *The Harbinger*, if America does not return to God, we can expect to see, with our own eyes, the end of the American age.

Chapter 22

The PROPHECIES *of* MESSIAH
in HEBREW SCRIPTURE

And Their Fulfillment: Yeshua

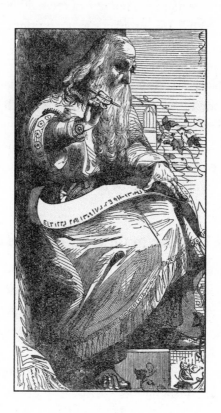

THE HEBREW SCRIPTURES give precise prophecies concerning the coming of Messiah. In all of Jewish history and world history there is no one who could be said to have fulfilled almost any of these. But there is one Jewish man, a rabbi, who fulfilled all of them.

Here are some of them:

- A child will be born to Israel and called the Mighty God, the Prince of Peace (Isa. 9:6–7).
- A child will be born to a virgin—and will be called "God with us" (Isa. 7:14).
- The Messiah will be born in the city of Bethlehem (Mic. 5:2).
- Messiah will be born as a descendant of David (Jer. 33:15).
- The Messiah, the shoot and root of Jesse, will be the one in whom the Gentiles will take refuge (Isa. 11:1, 10).
- The Lord will come to the Temple of Jerusalem (Mal. 3:1).
- The Messiah will be called the Son of God (Ps. 2:12; Prov. 30:4).
- The "stone" that the builders rejected will become the "chief cornerstone" (Ps. 118:22).
- The "Associate of God," the Shepherd of Israel, will be killed by the sword (Zech. 13:7).
- Messiah will be led into Jerusalem on a donkey (Zech. 9:9).
- The Book of Psalms gives a prophecy describing a specific crucifixion with the piercing of hands and feet and the casting lots for His garments (Ps. 22:14–18).
- The Lord says that in the end times, the people of Israel will "look on Me whom they *pierced*" (Zech. 12:10, emphasis added).
- Messiah will come before the Temple and city of Jerusalem are destroyed. Thus the Messiah had to come to Jerusalem before the year AD 70 (Dan. 9:24–26).
- Messiah will be "cut off" (die) in the city of Jerusalem before the year AD 70 (Dan. 9:24–26).
- He will be despised and rejected by men, even by His own people (Isa. 53:3).
- He will despised and treated as one who is judged by God (Isa. 53:4).

- He will be wounded for "our transgressions," bruised or crushed for "our iniquities [sins]" (Isa. 53:5).

- The punishment for our *shalom* (peace, well-being) will fall upon Him (Isa. 53:5).

- By His scourging we will be healed (Isa. 53:5).

- He does not open his mouth to protest as He is being afflicted and led to His death (Isa. 53:7).

- He will be led to his death as a lamb to the slaughter (Isa. 53:7).

- He will be killed (Isa. 53:8).

- His death and grave will be connected to wicked men, criminals, and with a rich man in His death (Isa. 53:9).

- His life will be an *asham*, a sacrifice that takes away guilt (Isa. 53:10).

- He will justify, make right, the many (Isa. 53:11).

- After His death He will be alive again (resurrection) and victorious (Isa. 53:10).

- God will make a new covenant, not like the old covenant that He made when He took Israel out of Egypt (Jer. 31:31).

- Messiah will become the light to the nations (Isa. 42:6).

- The child born in Israel, known as the Prince of Peace, will reign on David's throne, and of the spreading of His government there will be no end (Isa. 9:6–7).

Chapter 23

The ULTIMATE ISSUE

Yeshua, You, and Eternity

HEARING ABOUT THE real possibility of judgment can be scary. Some have asked, "What can I do? How can I be safe?" Some people seriously considered moving to what they consider to be safer locations.

But ultimately the issue is spiritual. No location in the world is far enough to keep the judgment of God out. The safest place you can be is not in the Midwest, in Canada, or on a remote island. The safest place you can be is the will of God.

In Hebrew the word for safety is *yeshua*. *Yesua* is the root word of the name *Yeshua*, which is also the real name of the one we know as Jesus. The safest place to be is not a matter of geography; it's a matter of the heart, a matter of faith, a matter of salvation. If your life is not in Jesus, Yeshua, salvation, then it is not saved. How can you be safe and saved from whatever lies ahead? You can only be safe in that which is safety and salvation—Yeshua, Jesus, the Messiah.

No matter what happens in a nation's judgment, the truth is, we will all one day stand in the light of God's judgment. There are only two ultimate roads. One road leads to God, and the other, away from Him. The first leads to heaven, eternal life, and the second to hell, eternal judgment for sin, eternal separation from God. Which road are you on? If you are not born again, you're on the wrong road and heading to the wrong destiny, the wrong eternity.

One day you will enter eternity. And it won't matter then what religion you were. The Bible says very little about religion. Nor will it matter how many good works you did. The Bible says that no one, on the basis of their works, can enter heaven. Then how can you be saved?

Messiah said this, "You must be born again" (John 3:7). The only way to be saved is by the new birth. It's a gift. No one is righteous enough to earn it. And no one is sinful enough to nullify it or the love of God. But as a gift, it must either be received or rejected. And to not accept it is the same as rejecting it.

How does one become born again? By receiving salvation, by receiving Yeshua, Jesus, by following Him, by putting your trust in the One who loved you, put His life in your place, died for your sins, bore your judgment, and overcame death to rise again that you might be saved. You receive His life given to you, and you give your life to Him. You turn away from the darkness and the sin, and you turn to following Him as His disciple.

Don't say you'll do it tomorrow. Tomorrow never comes. The Bible says, "Now is the accepted time; behold, now is the day of salvation"

(2 Cor. 6:2). You can only receive it now. Tomorrow isn't guaranteed. How far away is the Day of Judgment? How far away is heaven or hell? Just one heartbeat. It only takes one heartbeat to stop, and then come judgment and eternity. Every heartbeat is a gift from God. But every heartbeat is borrowed. Take the beating of your heart as the knocking of God's hand on the door of your life, saying, "Open up."

Where will you be a thousand years from now? You will be somewhere: either heaven or hell. If you're not sure, then you need to make it right with God. If you're not born again, now is the time you need to be. If you have been born again but haven't been living in His will, then now is the time to make it right. And if you have known God, but God is calling you to higher ground, then now is the time to commit to it and make it right.

Whatever you need to do, do it now. Whatever isn't right with God, get it right. Whatever is in your life but shouldn't be, lift it to God, be cleansed of it, repent of it, and leave it behind. Whatever is not in your life but should be, get it into your life. And whatever God is calling you to do, now is the time to do it.

Whatever it is, it can begin now, with a simple prayer from your heart to the heart of God. Do what you have to do. Do what God is calling you to do. For the distance from here to eternity is one heartbeat. And you never know which one will be your last. Whatever God is calling you to do—just do it.

Chapter 24

The STORY BEHIND *the* STORY

The Super Bowl, the Encounter, and the Stranger in the Airport (Special Feature From FrontLine)

The following is not intended to be a theological proposition as to how God typically works. There are extremes on every side of the issues. The message of *The Harbinger* is not based on nor does it weigh in on any of these issues concerning gifts or signs, but rather it is the revealing of the biblical template of national judgment now replaying in America, a message of warning and a calling to repentance, salvation, and revival. It transcends denominational lines. Nevertheless, the following is the true story of how this message went forth as a book to the nation.

א ת

THE PROPHECY OF Isaiah, central to *The Harbinger*, opens up with this introduction: "The Lord sends a message to Jacob, and it falls upon Israel...."

When God wanted a vital message, a warning, or an alarm to go forth to a nation, He made sure it happened. In the case of the message of *The Harbinger*, how did it end up going forth to America? The story is an amazing one and very much of the supernatural. It began with a Super Bowl.

A Supernatural Super Bowl

In 2008 David Tyree entered the field of play in the Super Bowl that pitted the New York Giants against the New England Patriots. At a key turning point of the game, he would jump up and, with one hand and in midair, grab the football thrown by Eli Manning, pin it down against his helmet, and return to the ground tackled. It would be called the greatest play in Super Bowl history.

But there was a story behind the play. What many people don't know is that David Tyree is a believer with a passion for the gospel. And before he went into the game, he had been given a prophetic word by another believer named Hubie Synn as to what would happen and that through this David Tyree would be given a platform to share the gospel. The word would be fulfilled in that catch. David Tyree would suddenly be lifted up into the spotlight. He would be given a platform with which to share the gospel. He would write a book. In that book he would mention Hubie Synn, the man who gave him the prophecy.

How to Go Forth

When Jonathan began writing *The Harbinger* in its present form, the words of the book flowed rapidly onto the computer almost as if the book had already been written before he wrote it. Within four months of writing in his spare time, *The Harbinger* was finished. But then he had a problem. He had no idea how it would be published. He had never written a book before. Nor had he approached any book publisher. Most books never get published, not to mention books by first-time writers. But he had no doubt that *The Harbinger* was of God and, as such, would go forth by God's hand.

The prayer in the Charlotte airport

At the end of the week in which he finished writing the book, Jonathan headed to Dallas where he was to speak at a Christian gathering there. The plane stopped in Charlotte, North Carolina. While sitting in the airport, waiting for the next flight, he was led to commit the future of *The Harbinger* to the Lord. He bowed his head and began to pray, knowing that *The Harbinger* was God's message, not man's, not his, and so it was for the Lord to bring forth the message—not by the strategies of man but by the hand of God for His purposes and His glory alone. So Jonathan committed the going forth of *The Harbinger* into the Lord's hands.

The stranger and the word

When he finished praying, he opened up his eyes, and a man was sitting to his left. The man turned to Jonathan and asked, "What's the good word?" The two started talking. All of a sudden the man began to speak in a different manner, telling Jonathan that he was going to publish a book, that this book was of the Lord, that God was about to do a great thing, and that it would change everything, his life, his ministry. He would be known across the land.

The man was not supposed to be there. But because of bad weather, his flight kept getting postponed until he was placed on Jonathan's flight and then sat down next to him. When he saw Jonathan and felt the leading to speak to him, he panicked, seeing that Jonathan looked Jewish; he thought he would not be open to anything he told him. But he felt constrained to speak.

Beyond that, the entire scene paralleled what Jonathan had just written in *The Harbinger* about a man sitting down in a public place. To his left sits a stranger who turns to him and initiates a conversation and then begins to give him a prophetic word that will ultimately lead him to write a book warning the nation of judgment and calling those who will hear to repentance and salvation. The man's name was Hubie Synn, the same one who gave the word concerning the Super Bowl and David Tyree.

The connection

Because he had given that word to David Tyree, and because David Tyree then wrote a book mentioning him, the man was brought in touch with the founder and CEO of Charisma Media, publisher of FrontLine books. He sent word to the CEO, Steve Strang, of his encounter at the Charlotte airport with a Jewish man bearing a message for America. Steve Strang then sent word to Jonathan that he heard of what happened at the airport, of his encounter, and of the message called *The Harbinger*. And though he had no idea what was in it, he was interested.

The Harbinger went on to be published and, from the first week of its release, became a national best seller. Yet it all began with a supernatural encounter with a mysterious stranger in the Charlotte airport.

Chapter 25

ABOUT *the* AUTHOR *of* The HARBINGER, JONATHAN CAHN

(Special Feature From FrontLine)

Ha Navi Gallery / AJMU

J ONATHAN CAHN, THE author of *The Harbinger,* was born into a Jewish home, of the line of Aaron. His father came from Germany having escaped the Holocaust. His mother's family came from Russia, having escaped the czar. Both his parents were scientists. As a boy he attended the synagogue from an early age. While in grade school he began to question what he was being taught. He perceived a disconnection between the God and faith of Bible times, where God appeared real and alive in people's lives and in the history of Israel, and what he saw in modern synagogue life. So at the age of eight he became an atheist.

UFOs, Science, the Occult, and Everything Else

His years as an atheist lasted until he was about thirteen years old when he became increasingly disillusioned with atheism. The idea that there was no reason behind existence provided no answers and rendered life meaningless. He began to search for answers, reading book after book on everything from science, religion, the supernatural, the occult, UFOs, and whatever else offered to provide answers. One day he picked up a book that he thought was on UFOs. It wasn't. It was *The Late Great Planet Earth* by Hal Lindsey. It was about the prophecies given in the Bible concerning the "last days," which were now coming to fulfillment in modern times.

The Messiah

The book led him to start considering and then searching the Bible. He picked up a copy of the Old Testament and began reading it. He found within it the prophecies of the coming Messiah, one who would be born in Bethlehem (Mic. 5:2), ride into Jerusalem on a donkey (Zech. 9:9), die for sins (Isa. 53), and become the hope of the Gentiles (Isa. 11). All sorts of ideas he thought were non-Jewish he now found speaking of the Jewish Messiah in the Hebrew Scriptures. After a long search he began to believe that only one person could be the Jewish Messiah: Yeshua, Jesus.

The Deal

But this faith was an intellectual assent rather than a heart-based or life-changing decision. His life as a typical teenager remained unchanged. He began to tell his friends about what he was discovering. To his surprise, his friend's lives began to change as they began to turn their lives to God. Jonathan began coming to the realization that it wasn't enough to believe in one's mind that Jesus was the Messiah.

He knew that although his belief was correct, his life wasn't. And if he found himself face-to-face with God, he would be on the wrong side of judgment. A decision was needed. He had to decide to follow what he knew was right, to turn his heart to God, to commit his life, and to live as a disciple.

The problem was—he didn't want to do any of these things. He believed that if you turned your life to God, it would be tantamount to joining a monastery. You would give up every good thing about life. And he wasn't ready to do that. So he made a deal with God. The deal was this: if God would grant him a long life, he would turn his life over to God to follow Him…when he was about to die, on his death bed.

Crossing the Railroad Tracks

Soon after making that deal, Jonathan was almost killed—twice. The first incident involved a car accident, with his car swerving out of control in and out of lanes of oncoming traffic. It appeared a miracle that he wasn't killed.

The second near-death experience was even more dramatic. Jonathan was nineteen, and he was driving a Ford Pinto at night, approaching a railroad track. The intersection was a dangerous one. There was no physical barrier stopping cars from the path of the train. The road was rough so that one might be on the track without realizing it.

He saw a light going on and off. He assumed it was the warning light signaling the coming of the train. But other cars on the other side of the street were crossing the track. He thought perhaps the train had already passed or that the light was broken. He moved his car forward to make sure. He looked to his left and saw a light. The light didn't appear to be moving. It was the light of the approaching train. It didn't seem to be moving because it was coming head-on.

Jonathan was on the track—but didn't realize it. At one point, he thought that to be safe, it would be wise to back up. But now another car was in back of him shining its headlights into his rearview mirror. He couldn't tell how much space he had. He backed up just slightly and was sure he was safe. He wasn't. He was still in the path of the train.

After the Crash—the Mountaintop

The train approached the intersection and plowed into the Ford Pinto. The metal in the car became like aluminum foil. The only thing Jonathan could do in those moments was call out to God. The car was destroyed, but he didn't get a scratch on his body. The event made headlines in the local paper, not only because of the crash but also because he didn't get a scratch. After emerging from the collision, he pondered the fact that it was only a matter of inches that separated his life from eternity, from judgment, from heaven or hell. He remembered the deal he had made with God and realized that his deathbed could come much sooner than he had bargained for.

Confronted with the reality of death and eternity, he again spoke to God—now to renegotiate the deal. He wouldn't wait until the time of his death to accept the Lord, which he now realized could come at any time. Instead, he would accept the Lord and start following the Lord…when he turned twenty.

About eight months later, on his twentieth birthday, coming to God as a man whose contract had run out and not knowing exactly what to do or how to do it, Jonathan got into his car and drove up a mountain overlooking the Hudson River. When he reached the top, he found a rock on which to kneel down. There on that mountaintop he committed his life to following God.

The Calling

Jonathan was in college, majoring in history, when his life changed. Outside of college he worked as a night watchman, doing schoolwork and studying the Scriptures. Soon he realized he was called into full-time ministry. He was asked to lead a Bible study, which he did for years. He started an outreach to the homeless of New York City, bringing them food and the Word of God. Upon graduating from college, he decided not to go on to postgraduate work but to find the calling the Lord had for him. He asked the Lord to give him a job that the Lord would have done. He was given a job working with disabled children.

Entering Into Ministry/Beth Israel

At the same time he was asked to help start an outreach called Beth Israel. He agreed to do it on the condition that those who asked him knew that his capacity in helping out would be temporary, subject to the time he would enter full-time ministry. A few years later the leader of the outreach left the ministry. Jonathan was approached to take the position. He was reluctant but eventually accepted.

When he accepted the position of leadership, there were about thirty-five people in the congregation. Soon it doubled, then tripled. The church in which the meetings took place asked the congregation to find their own place. But there was no money. One day a man showed up and told Jonathan that the Lord had told him to give Jonathan a gift of $150,000. With this, the congregation purchased its first building. Within a short time and much growth, the new building became too small for services. After much searching, another building was found, ten times the size of the first. During this time Beth Israel became one of the largest Messianic congregations in the world. Years later the congregation moved again, to a building three times larger than the last.

The Jerusalem Center/
Beth Israel and Hope of the World

Beth Israel, or the Jerusalem Center, is a Messianic ministry, in that it is made up of Jew and Gentile, people of all nations, together in Messiah. It is known for restoring the original biblical Jewish flavor of the New Testament faith. With worship services on Friday nights and Sunday mornings, and with celebrations of the holy days of the Bible, the Jerusalem Center in Wayne, New Jersey, has become one of the largest Messianic congregations in the world. It is here that Jonathan regularly teaches the Word and where he first shared the message of *The Harbinger*.

From the Jerusalem Center Jonathan leads the world outreach ministry called Hope of the World, dedicated to spreading the Word of God to the unreached of the world and to helping the poor and needy of all nations.

Jonathan's teachings are known for their profound and prophetic nature and for revealing the deep mysteries of biblical truth. His messages are heard around the nation and world through radio and television. He is greatly sought after as a speaker. He has ministered to audiences numbering in the tens of thousands, even millions, in places like India, Latin America, and Africa.

To get in touch with Jonathan's ministry, see the contact information at the end of the book.

■ CHAPTER 26 ■

A GUIDED TOUR
OF *THE HARBINGER*

א ת

THE HARBINGER TOUR

1 Begin your Harbinger Tour at Battery Park, located at the very southern end of the island of Manhattan. Looking out at the water's edge to the southwest, you can see the Statue of Liberty. Known as the "gateway" of America, this is the corridor where the second plane breached America's hedge of protection on September 11, 2001. It was also here in *The Harbinger* that the prophet met Nouriel to unlock the mystery of the First Harbinger, the opening sign of national judgment—the Breach, when an enemy was allowed to make a strike on the land. (Refer to *The Harbinger* chapter 4, "The First Harbinger: The Breach.")

2 From Battery Park, walk north on Broadway until you arrive at Trinity Wall Street. This is the "mother church" of St. Paul's Chapel. There you can see the Trinity Root, a sculpture of the roots of the fallen Sycamore of Ground Zero, the Sixth Harbinger. The statue is normally displayed in full view outside the church's southern courtyard. During times of construction, it can be partially obscured from view. It was under a sycamore tree  that America began its rise to financial superpower, as the Buttonwood Agreement was signed under a type of sycamore tree. The same sign of the sycamore reappeared on 9/11 but is now struck down. So today at the end of Wall Street—marked by the sign of the sycamore from its beginning—rests the symbol of a sycamore uprooted. (Refer to chapter 16, "The Uprooted.")

3 From Trinity Church, turn right and walk down Wall Street to the New York Stock Exchange. In the seventeenth century, the island of Manhattan served as a trading post for the Dutch. To protect themselves from perceived threats, the Dutch built a wall, hence the name Wall Street. When the Dutch  lost Manhattan to the British, the wall was torn down but the name remained. Today it has become the center of America's financial strength. It was also here on Wall Street that in 1792 twenty-four merchants signed the Buttonwood (sycamore) Agreement to begin what would become known as the New York Stock Exchange, and launch America's rise to global financial superpower. It is down this street that the prophet leads Nouriel as he opens up the mystery of the buttonwood. (Refer to chapter 16, " The Uprooted.")

4 Across from the New York Stock Exchange you'll find Federal Hall, where America as we know it came into existence on April 30, 1789, when New York City was  the nation's capital. On the front steps of Federal Hall you can view the statue of George Washington that marks the spot where he put his hand on a Bible and was sworn in as the nation's first president. It was also here that Washington gave a prophetic warning to the nation concerning what would happen if America ever turned away from God. In *The Harbinger* this is where the prophet leads Nouriel as he shares the secret of the Mystery Ground. (Refer to chapter 19, "The Mystery Ground.")

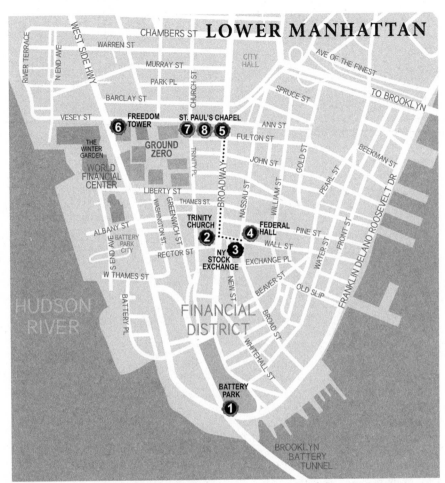

LOWER MANHATTAN

From Federal Hall, Washington and America's first fully formed government—the new administration, and the members of the House of Representatives and Senate—walked to an appointed spot to dedicate the new government and the new nation into the hands of God. Retrace this journey. Walk back up Wall Street to Broadway, then turn right on Broadway and walk past Zuccotti Park on up to St. Paul's Chapel. (Note path marked on the map.) This is the nation's consecration ground, the place where America's future was dedicated to God on its first day. St. Paul's Chapel is

the oldest building in New York City in continuous use. In the days of Washington's inauguration, its entrance was on the opposite side, away from Broadway, on the side facing its courtyard and what is now Ground Zero. In *The Harbinger*, the prophet leads Nouriel here and then around the back by the courtyard. (Refer to chapter 19, "The Mystery Ground.")

Walk around to the back of the chapel. There you'll glimpse the ancient courtyard and cemetery inside the black iron fence. Look just beyond the courtyard, and you will see Ground Zero. This is where the Twin Towers once stood and where calamity came to America, in keeping with the ancient principle that calamity returns to the nation's consecration ground. Two reflecting ponds sit where the Third Harbinger: The

Photo courtesy of Margie Bibb

Fallen Bricks once rested. And out of this site rises the Fourth Harbinger, The Tower. At over 100 stories, Freedom Tower (now called One World Trade Center) will be one of the world's tallest skyscrapers when construction is complete. The Fifth Harbinger: The Gazit Stone—or Freedom Stone—was dedicated as the cornerstone of Freedom Tower in 2004. But when the tower was redesigned, the stone, cut from the Adirondack Mountains, was removed. At the time of this writing, it sits outside Innovative Stone in Hauppauge, New York, about 50 miles away. Here also in the ruins of Ground Zero once stood a 20-foot steel cross. Forged out of the fallen tower, the Ground Zero Cross was stationed near the southeast corner. In *The Harbinger*, Nouriel gazes at this site, at first almost in disbelief, as the pieces of the mystery begin to come together. (Refer to chapter 19, "The Mystery Ground," chapter 21, "Eternity," chapter 7, "The Third Harbinger: The Fallen Bricks," chapter 8, "The Fourth Harbinger: The Tower," and chapter 9, "The Fifth Harbinger: The Gazit Stone.")

7 From Ground Zero, walk back to St. Paul's Chapel. Enter through the iron gates into the courtyard. Turn left and in the northwest corner of the courtyard you will see the place where the Sycamore of Ground Zero stood and was struck down on 9/11. The Sycamore was removed from the place where it had fallen and put on display for a time on the east side of the courtyard. In its place was lowered the Erez Tree, a Norwegian Spruce, a sister tree to the Cedar of Lebanon, in accordance with the vow of ancient Israel. At the time of this writing, it still stands there on the northwest corner of the courtyard as the Ground Zero Tree of Hope. This is where Nouriel and the prophet gaze at the soil of America's consecration ground and the soil of the Sixth and Seventh Harbingers. (Refer to chapter 19, "The Mystery Ground," chapter 10, "The Sixth Harbinger: The Sycamore," and chapter 11, "The Seventh Harbinger: The Erez Tree.")

8 Now enter Paul's Chapel and stand in the place where America was dedicated to God on its first day. President Washington and all the nation's early government leaders met together to pray for the Lord's blessing on the nation. Inside the chapel, you can see the pew where George Washington regularly prayed. Above

Photo by Roger Bilisoly

the pew is a small golden plaque that records the words of Washington's prayer asking the Lord for His "holy protection" on America. One can also find one of the earliest depictions of the nation's Great Seal. Note one small difference between the seal we have today—instead of an eagle is a turkey. On the eastern side of the chapel is a depiction of the Ten Commandments. (Refer to chapter 19, "The Mystery Ground.")

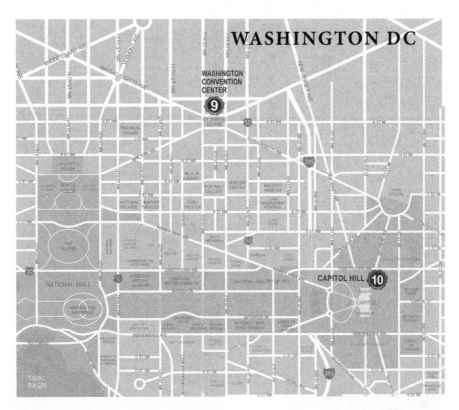

WASHINGTON DC

9 The Eighth and Ninth Harbingers take place in Washington DC. In Washington, you can visit the Walter E. Washington Convention Center at 801 Mount Vernon Place Northwest. That is where on September 11, 2004, Sen. John Edwards gave The Utterance when he quoted from Isaiah 9:10 during a Congressional Black Caucus Prayer Breakfast. (Refer to chapter 12, "The Eighth Harbinger: The Utterance.")

in the House Chamber. This is also the place President Obama entered on February 24, 2009, to

make his own declaration that paralleled the ancient vow. In front of the Capitol building, on the side overlooking the Washington Mall, are the steps of the Western Terrace, where America's presidents are sworn into office. It was here that Nouriel and the prophet stood gazing out at the Washington Mall. (Refer to chapter 13, "The Ninth Harbinger: The Prophecy" and chapter 18, "The Third Witness.")

10 The Ninth Harbinger is The Prophecy, spoken September 12, 2001, by Senate Majority Leader Tom Daschle at the Capitol building. This was done before a Joint Session of Congress

The Capitol steps would be a perfect place to pray for America's future, that the nation would turn back to God and experience a spiritual awakening.

NOTES

Chapter 1
The Harbinger: An Introduction

1. H. D. M. Spence and Joseph S. Exell, eds., *The Pulpit Commentary*, vol. 10, Isaiah (Peabody, MA: Hendrickson Publishers, 1985), 178.

Chapter 2
Ancient Israel: The Rise and the Apostasy

1. Gonzalo Báez-Camargo, *Archeological Commentary on the Bible* (New York: Doubleday and Company, 1984), 55.

2. Merrill F. Unger, *Archeology and the Old Testament* (Grand Rapids, MI: Zondervan, 1954), 279.

3. Raymond Brown, *The Message of Deuteronomy* (Downers Grove, IL: InterVarsity Academic, 1993), 146.

4. Robert Jamieson, A. R. Fausset, and David Brown, *Commentary Critical and Explanatory on the Whole Bible* (New York: S. S. Scranton and Company, 1871), s.v. "Ezekiel 16:22." Viewed online at Christian Classics Ethereal Library.

Chapter 3
America's Rise and Fall

1. John Winthrop, *Winthrop's History of N.E.*, vol. 1, 52–53, as quoted in Robert Charles Winthrop, *Life and Letters of John Winthrop, 1630 to 1649* (Boston: Ticknor and Fields, 1867), 14. Viewed online at Google Books.

2. Gabriel Sivan, *The Bible and Civilization* (New York: Quadrangle/New York Times Book Company, 1974), 236.

3. David H. Stern, *Jewish New Testament Commentary* (n.p.: Jewish New Testament Publications 1992), comment on John 7:2, as referenced in Mario Seiglie, "Is Thanksgiving Rooted in a Biblical Festival?", *The Good News*, November–December 2010, http://www.ucg.org/holidays-and-holy-days/thanksgiving-rooted-biblical-festival/ (accessed October 20, 2012).

4. Alan B. Bernstein, *Guide to Your Career* (New York: The Princeton Review, 2004), 445. Viewed online at Google Books.

5. GreatSeal.com, "First Great Seal Committee—July/August 1776," http://www.greatseal.com/committees/firstcomm/ (accessed October 20, 2012); also, GreatSeal.com, "Benjamin Franklin's Great Seal Design," http://www.greatseal.com/committees/firstcomm/reverse.html (accessed October 20, 2012).

6. Donald S. Lutz, "The Relative Influence of European Writers on Late Eighteenth-Century American Political Thought," *American Political Science Review* 78 (March 1984): 189–197.

7. John T. Woolley and Gerhard Peters, *The American Presidency Project (online)*, "Ronald Reagan: Proclamation 5018—Year of the Bible, 1983, February 3, 1983," http://www.presidency.ucsb.edu/ws/?pid=40728 (accessed October 18, 2012). See the same quote in a proclamation from President George H. W. Bush on February 22, 1990, "International Year of Bible Reading," in *Code of Federal Regulations* (Washington DC: U.S. Government Printing Office, 1991), 21.

8. John T. Woolley and Gerhard Peters, *The American Presidency Project (online)*, "Harry S. Truman: Address Before the Attorney General's Conference on Law Enforcement Problems, February 15, 1950," http://www.presidency.ucsb.edu/ws/?pid=13707 (accessed October 18, 2012).

9. John Adams, "To the Officers of the First Brigade of the Third Division of the Militia of Massachusetts, 11 October 1798," in *The Works of John Adams, Second President of the United States*, vol. 9 (Boston: Little, Brown and Company, 1854), 228. Viewed online at Google Books.

10. John Rodgers, "'The Dominion of Providence Over the Works of Men,' A Sermon Preached at Princeton, on the 17th of May, 1776," in *The Works of the Rev. John Witherspoon*, vol. 2 (Philadelphia: William W. Woodward, 1800), 424. Viewed online at Google Books.

Chapter 4
The Harbingers: The Breach to the Gazit Stone

1. George Roux, *Ancient Iraq* (New York: Penguin, 1964, 1992), 190.

2. Since the original Hebrew of Isaiah 9:10 contains greater meaning than any single translation can render, throughout this book the words of this particular verse are translated and expounded upon directly from the original Hebrew.

3. Jamieson, Fausset, and Brown, *Commentary Critical and Explanatory on the Whole Bible*, s.v. "Isaiah 9:10."

4. *The Interpreter's Bible*, vol. 5 (New York: Abingdon Press, 1956), 235.

5. Spence and Exell, eds., *The Pulpit Commentary*, vol. 10, Isaiah, 178.

6. TheModernTribune.com: "Kerry: 'We Must Build a New World Trade Center—and Build American Resolve for a New War on Terrorism,'" speech delivered on the floor of the US Senate, September 12, 2001, as quoted in *The Modern Tribune Online*, http://www.themodern tribune.com/john_kerry_speech_after_9_11_-_rebuild_america_and_ the_world_trade_center.htm (accessed October 18, 2012).

7. "Remarks, Governor George E. Pataki, Laying of the Cornerstone for Freedom Tower, July 4, 2004," http://www.renewnyc.com/content/ speeches/Gov_speech_Freedom_Tower.pdf (accessed October 18, 2012).

8. *English Translation of the Greek Septuagint Bible*, compiled from the translation by Sir Lancelot C. L. Brenton, 1851, s.v. "Isaiah 9:10," http://www.ecmarsh.com/lxx/Esaias/index.htm (accessed October 18, 2012).

Chapter 5
The Harbingers: The Sycamore to the Prophecy

1. John T. Woolley and Gerhard Peters, *The American Presidency Project (online)*, "John Edwards: Remarks to the Congressional Black Caucus Prayer Breakfast, September 11, 2004," http://www.presidency .ucsb.edu/ws/index.php?pid=84922#axzz1M02bgo9D (accessed October 18, 2012).

2. Ibid.

3. Ibid.

4. Ibid.

5. Ibid.

6. Washington File, "Senate Majority Leaders Daschle Expresses Sorrow, Resolve," September 12, 2001, http://wfile.ait.org.tw/wf -archive/2001/010913/epf407.htm (accessed October 18, 2012).

7. Ibid.

Chapter 6
The Isaiah 9:10 Effect

1. ShropshireStar.com, "9/11: 'The Root' of the Financial Crisis," *Shropshire Star*, October 28, 2008, http://www.shropshirestar.com/ news/2008/10/28/911-the-root-of-the-financial-crisis (accessed October 18, 2012).

2. CNBC.com, "House of Cards: Origins of the Financial Crisis Then and Now," slideshow, http://www.cnbc.com/id/28993790/Origins_of _the_Financial_Crisis_Then_and_Now_Slideshow (accessed October 18, 2012).

Chapter 8
The Mystery of the Shemitah

1. *Newsweek*, "Did Lehman's Fall Matter?," May 17, 2009, http:// www.thedailybeast.com/newsweek/2009/05/17/did-lehman-s-fall -matter.html (accessed October 18, 2012).

2. Alexandra Twin, "Stocks Crushed," CNNMoney.com, September 29, 20008, http://money.cnn.com/2008/09/29/markets/markets _newyork/index.htm (accessed October 18, 2012).

Chapter 9
The Three Witnesses

1. WhiteHouse.gov, "Remarks of President Barack Obama—as Pre-pared for Delivery to Joint Session of Congress, Tuesday, February 24, 2009," http://www.whitehouse.gov/the_press_office/Remarks-of -President-Barack-Obama-Address-to-Joint-Session-of-Congress (accessed October 18, 2012).

2. Gary V. Smith, *The New American Commentary* (Nashville: Broadman and Holman, 2007), 246, s.v. "Isaiah 9."

3. WhiteHouse.gov, "Remarks of President Barack Obama—as Pre-pared for Delivery to Joint Session of Congress, Tuesday, February 24, 2009."

4. Ibid.

5. Washington File, "Senate Majority Leader Daschle Expresses Sorrow, Resolve," September 12, 2001, http://wfile.ait.org.tw/wf -archive/2001/010913/epf407.htm (accessed October 18, 2012), emphasis added.

6. WhiteHouse.gov, "Remarks of President Barack Obama—as Pre-pared for Delivery to Joint Session of Congress, Tuesday, February 24, 2009," emphasis added.

Chapter 10
The Mystery Ground

1. Avalon Project at Yale Law School, "First Inaugural Address of George Washington, The City of New York, Thursday, April 30, 1789,"

http://avalon.law.yale.edu/18th_century/wash1.asp (accessed October 18, 2012).

2. Ibid.

3. Historical Marker Database, "On This Site in Federal Hall," http://www.hmdb.org/Marker.asp?Marker=13734 (accessed October 18, 2012).

Chapter 14
The Harbinger: The Story and the Characters

1. As quoted in BibleTools.org, "Annas," from *International Standard Bible Encyclopedia*, http://www.bibletools.org/index.cfm/fuseaction/Def.show/RTD/ISBE/ID/541/Annas.htm (accessed October 21, 2012).

Chapter 16
Who Is "the Prophet"?

1. Jonathan Cahn, *The Harbinger* (Lake Mary, FL: FrontLine, 2012), 10.

2. Ibid., 24.

3. Jeremiah 36:5–6.

4. Cahn, *The Harbinger*, 246–247.

Chapter 17
Who Is Nouriel?

1. Stephen Mihm, "Dr. Doom," *New York Times*, August 15, 2008, http://www.nytimes.com/2008/08/17/magazine/17pessimist-t.html (accessed October 21, 2012).

2. Cahn, *The Harbinger*, 246.

Chapter 18
The Seals (and the Seal Behind the Seals)

1. Ibid., 239.

2. Ibid., 240.

3. BibleHistory.net, "Jeremiah's Scribe—'Baruch,'" Old Testament, chapter 25, http://www.biblehistory.net/Baruch_Jeremiah.pdf (accessed October 21, 2012).

Chapter 19
Frequently Asked Questions About
The Harbinger and Jonathan Cahn

1. As quoted in Joseph Farah, "'The Harbinger': Fact, Fiction, Confusion, Reality," *WND* Commentary, August 24, 2012, http://www.wnd.com/2012/08/the-harbinger-fact-fiction-confusion-reality/ (accessed October 21, 2012).

2. J. Adams, "Jonathan Cahn: The Harbinger" *The Spirit of Truth Blog*, April 1, 2012, http://www.thespiritoftruth.blogspot.com/2012/04/jonathan-cahn-harbinger.html.

The Harbinger: The Ancient Mystery That Holds the Secret of America's Future (FrontLine/Charisma Media)

Available wherever books are sold; also available as an audiobook

The Harbinger Companion With Study Guide (FrontLine/Charisma Media)

Available wherever books are sold

The Harbinger: The Full Revelation (eight-disc album available on DVDs or CDs)

1. The Harbinger I
2. The Isaiah 9:10 Effect
3. The Uprooted
4. The Mystery of the Shemitah I
5. The Mystery of the Shemitah II
6. The Three Witnesses
7. The Mystery Ground
8. The Harbinger II: Summation

Available from TheHarbingerWebsite.org

Additional teachings

- The City on the Hill
- If My People
- The American Prophecies
- The Harbinger Continues
- The Yoma Mysteries
- The Eden Mysteries
- The Infinity Solution
- Azazel
- The Mystery Age and the Eighth Day
- Entering Your Prophetic Destiny
- And more…

Available through Jonathan's ministry:

Hope of the World
P. O. Box 1111
Lodi, NJ 07644
www.hopeoftheworld.org

FREE NEWSLETTERS
TO HELP EMPOWER YOUR LIFE

Why subscribe today?

❏ **DELIVERED DIRECTLY TO YOU.** All you have to do is open your inbox and read.

❏ **EXCLUSIVE CONTENT.** We cover the news overlooked by the mainstream press.

❏ **STAY CURRENT.** Find the latest court rulings, revivals, and cultural trends.

❏ **UPDATE OTHERS.** Easy to forward to friends and family with the click of your mouse.

CHOOSE THE E-NEWSLETTER THAT INTERESTS YOU MOST:

- Christian news
- Daily devotionals
- Spiritual empowerment
- And much, much more

SIGN UP AT: **http://freenewsletters.charismamag.com**

8178